Peter Michel: Krishnamurti—Love and Freedom
Approaching a Mystery

Peter Michel

—Krishnamurti—
Love and Freedom

Approaching a Mystery

Bluestar
Communications
Woodside, California

This book was originally written in German. In translating the text to English, the editors have attempted to find and include the original English language source for all quoted material. Any cases where this was not possible are indicated in a footnote.

The editors would like to thank the many people who provided valuable assistance in this task, in particular Scott Forbes and Kishhore Khairnar, The Brockwood Park Krishnamurti Educational Center, London, England, and the staff of both the Olcott Library & Research Center, Wheaton, Illinois, and The Krishnamurti Library, The Krishnamurti Foundation of America, Ojai, California.

Translated by Petra Michel

First published in German under the title
Krishnamurti—Freiheit und Liebe
Annäherung an ein Geheimnis
by Aquamarin Verlag, Grafing, Germany 1992

This translation:
© 1995 Bluestar Communications Corporation
44 Bear Glenn
Woodside, CA 94062
Tel: 800-6-Bluestar

First printing 1995

ISBN: 1-885394-00-4

Printed in China

Contents

Where there is sorrow there cannot be love.

Krishnamurti, July 17, 1985, in Saanen.

Preface

To write a biography—and especially one about Krishnamurti—urges the author of that biography to step back totally behind the person he wants to write about. He should attempt to become a kind of 'invisible historical observer' in the background of events or at most to appear in the book as an impersonal 'one.' I do not intend to follow in this tradition and I explain my reasons for that choice in the following.

I was acquainted with the works of Krishnamurti for over a decade. I knew about his life, had read some of his books and had even written about his teaching[1]. For all those years he had been a stranger to me, he had no particular fascination for me. I had considered his talks and discussions as merely intellectual and had not found the 'inspiration' (a comment often made regarding Krishnamurti.) Nonetheless this mysterious figure existed in a niche of my consciousness, with his highly unusual 'messianic' past, a figure I saw as a kind of 'Sphinx of the 20th Century.' Therefore, when in the early summer of 1985 I read the announcement of his annual talks in Saanen, which I had not noticed for years (why not?...), the advertisement created an irresistible impulse within me to go to Saanen that June.

The encounter with Krishnamurti during that indescribably beautiful summer, in a sunbathed, light-filled Swiss mountain area, left its mark on my life for several years. I was touched by a reality that manifested itself through that frail, filigree person on his simple wooden seat, a reality which can only be characterized by the word 'holy,' but a 'holy' that is free of its modern sweetness and reduced to its original purity.

In her book on Krishnamurti, Pupul Jayakar writes about her first meeting with him that she also experienced as deeply moving. "Krishnamurti entered the room silently, and my senses exploded; I had a sudden intense perception of immensity and radiance. He filled the room with his presence, and for an instant I was devastated."[2] Her second sentence describes an inner experience that was quite similar to my own. The tent in which Krishnamurti was talking no longer reflected a limited reality. Here, while talking in time and space he carried the person who opened himself deeply to a sphere of being beyond both time and space. I cannot recall another time in my life when I have listened more intensely than during this summer in Saanen. Yet only with great difficulty could I repeat the content of the talks. When I published a transcript of the talks two years later,[3] I read an unknown text and was amazed how much it had moved me at the time. And to me this seems to be the real mystery. My transformation occurred less through the words than through the energy that emanated from this inconspicuous person sitting in the chair who said about himself in each and every talk: "K. is not important."[4]

Often after the talks, it took me hours to re-integrate the normalcy of Saanen and Gstaad into my own world. In addition, I listened to those talks by Krishnamurti at a time of difficult personal relationships that were overshadowing my life. The shadows dissolved during those days and in the weeks following the talks, like storm clouds giving way to the sun of a bright morning. I realized in those hours and days what Krishnamurti meant when he said he wanted to set every human being free, "totally and unconditionally." Perhaps I needed this personal encounter (and touch) to understand his message deep within myself and then to be able to live it—his books alone did not give me that message.

Freedom and Love is the title of this biography. I have already mentioned freedom but what about love? Again I refer to Pupul Jayakar. In the final sentence of the preface of her biography she lets her mind wander over the many years she and Krishnamurti spent together and writes: "And yet in his presence one felt the bounty of an infinite concern."[5] This emanation, which I sensed as his boundless love for all creation, cannot be conveyed by the written word—one must encounter it in person. It may sometimes shine through, if the discussion leads in the right direction, as it did once when I met Pupul Jayakar at my home.[6] Our discussions focused on Krishnamurti and during this intense dialog we both sensed a little bit of the 'spirit of Krishnamurti' himself.

This love, this 'ceaseless compassion,' can be experienced in Krishnamurti's *Notebook*, particularly in his description of nature.[7] I recall how deeply I was touched when I read his notes about the weeks he spent in the Giant Forest of Sequoia National Park, California. Anyone who has sat at the feet of those majestic trees and who has meditated in this forest cathedral must realize from Krishnamurti's description what an intense union he had formed with nature. A union of love. Sometimes, when I read his most personal thoughts, I sense he believed that nature, in its purity, understood him better than a humanity dominated by ego ever could.

Krishnamurti insisted, even hours before his death, that nobody had his permission to speak as an authority on his works or to speak in his name. His thoughts, he said, should speak for themselves and should not be compromised by an odd 'guru-image.' He did not dissolve the 'Order of the Star,' did not decline his 'Messiah Office' only to be confronted with yet another Krishnamurti cult. He regarded the organizations that were formed around his person as worldly ordering and administrative bodies, never as some kind of keepers-of-the-grail for Krishnamurti teachings. Taking all this into account, a book about his life and his thoughts cannot claim any authority. It can only be an 'approach to the mystery.'

During a discussion with Susunaga Weeraperuma, who had talked to him about writing a book, Krishnamurti defined some basic rules which were to be followed if somebody intended to write a book about him. He said to Weeraperuma: "It is very simple. You must write in the light of your own understanding. Don't read into the teachings what is not intended. This means that you are no longer influenced by the various ideas, beliefs and experiences that have conditioned your outlook on life. When writing about the teachings, can you not state that you are only investigating them? Both you and your readers are going on a voyage of discovery together. Neither of you is sure what exactly K meant by a certain statement. Therefore you can never say, 'This is what K meant.' All you can say is, 'Probably this is what K meant.' It is good to use words like 'perhaps' and 'probably' because they introduce an element of doubt in the mind of the reader. Sir, if you do that you will not run the risk of becoming a misinterpreter."[8] In the following chapters, I try to act according to Krishnamurti's wishes. I attempt to approach Krishnamurti along with you, the reader. Many people have already made an effort to do so and you will hear several voices in the following pages. All of these people were inspired by meeting this unusual human being—this Jiddu Krishnamurti.

If this biography can help the reader to experience freedom and love, as I did through those meetings with Krishnamurti, my highest expectations will certainly have been met. Only in freedom and in love, and only alone, can one realize the awakening to the light and the resurrection from the cross of matter. Krishnamurti saw himself as a way-shower in this process, but who would be so ignorant, using his own words, "to adore the way shower?" One reads the message and moves on.

Peter Michel
Good Friday, 1991

Part 1
THE LIFE

I. The Discovery

On May 12, 1895, Krishnamurti was born in Madanapalle, a small village in Andhra Pradesh, a southern province of India. Reports of his exact date of birth are somewhat varied due to an interpretation of Indian astrology, where days are measured from four o'clock in the morning until the next morning at the same time. In western notation, Krishnamurti was born that same day at thirty minutes past midnight. By the next day, one of the notable astrologers in the area (Kumara Shrow-Thulu) had made his chart and predicted a great future for the young Krishnamurti. Even before Krishnamurti was born, his mother, Sanjeevamma, had a premonition that her eighth child would be an exceptional being. (Like Krishna, Krishnamurti was an eighth child.) For this reason Krishnamurti was born in the Puja Room, contradicting Indian tradition. This preferential treatment is like a symbol for his life, which has always been shaped by the exceptions, and Krishnamurti has always had people around him who were looking after him constantly.9 The story about Krishnamurti's discovery by Charles W. Leadbeater has been told many times. The best source regarding the young Krishnamurti and the events between 1909 and 1911 is the little book by Russell Balfour-Clarke, *The Boyhood of J. Krishnamurti*. From the first month of Krishnamurti's entrance into the Theosophical Society, Clarke was both his English teacher and his companion.

The exact date of Krishnamurti's discovery by Leadbeater cannot be determined today. However, Annie Besant did not mention Krishnamurti before she left Adyar on April 22, 1909,

17

and so the event probably took place sometime in May, 1909. As Pupul Jayakar points out, it does not seem particularly important whether his discovery by Leadbeater was a spontaneous insight or followed observation over several days. However, all reports are unanimous that Leadbeater was impressed by Krishnamurti's aura, which showed no sign whatsoever of selfishness. This observation has been reported by all biographers of Krishnamurti without question. Contrary to this point of view, the Austrian, John Cordes, who was living in Adyar then and was in close contact with both Leadbeater and Krishnamurti, said that Leadbeater had told him that he had actually recognized Krishnamurti for his *causal body*.[10] This is particularly important because theosophical anthropology states that the causal body is carried over from one incarnation to the next and that in a certain way it represents the *soul* of a human being. Therefore, according to Cordes, Leadbeater did not base his choice on the personality of Krishnamurti but on his spirit-soul being. This point is considered in more detail later, when we try to answer the question: 'Who was Krishnamurti?'

After Leadbeater had learned about Krishnamurti's education and private life, he soon recognized that it was necessary to place him into the care of the Theosophical Society. In spite of the numerous differences between Krishnamurti and Leadbeater in later life, Krishnamurti always recognized that his 'discovery' by Leadbeater had saved his life. By the early fifties only one of the fourteen children in his former group was still living—Krishnamurti.[11] For the assessment of this phenomenon, it is not important that Leadbeater, due to his conception of the world at that time, needed the pure body of a high-cast Brahman for his Messiah ideals.[12]

Leadbeater's research on the former lives of Krishnamurti is far more interesting, although it is a work

18

that has been strongly criticized. Those former lifetimes show a deep connection to India and an incarnation under the direct influence of the historical Buddha Gautama.[13] This is not the right context in which to judge clairvoyant research on reincarnation but one can state that despite his undoubted cosmo-political spirituality, Krishnamurti felt a life-long and deep connection to Indian mysticism and to Sanskrit, a language he enjoyed chanting. Of all historical religious figures it was Buddha who attracted him the most.

It is impossible to discuss the discovery of Krishnamurti without referring to the shimmering personality of Charles W. Leadbeater. No other person in the history of the Theosophical Society has brought so much controversy upon himself. Whether Krishnamurti really said that Leadbeater was evil[14] is a topic that is not addressed in this book. Pupul Jayakar reports an event from the year 1981 when, for the first time in forty-seven years, Krishnamurti entered the property of the Theosophical Society in Madras and came across a picture of Leadbeater. "Suddenly, he stopped before a large photograph of Leadbeater which hung on the wall. 'This was not there in my time,' he said. Radha Burnier said it had been placed there many years later. For minutes Krishnaji stood before the portrait, gazing at it; then suddenly he raised his hand and said, 'Pax, pax.' Then he turned to Radha Burnier and walked out of the room."[15]

Having spent three quarters of a century near Leadbeater, Mary Lutyens made the following positive remark: "I then believed implicitly in his clairvoyance; I do not disbelieve in it today. An extraordinary man, a man of charm and magnetism and with an apparent sincerity it was hard to doubt, to me he remains an enigma."[16] Balfour-Clarke supports Mary Lutyen's point of view and regards the accusations of Leadbeater's possible homosexuality as incorrect.[17] One should take into account that Leadbeater gave his advice regarding sexual matters during a time of late-Victorian prudery. Later, Mary Lutyens realized that Leadbeater was ahead of his times in this regard. "Nothing has ever been proven against Leadbeater. He never for a moment denied advocating masturbation as a prophylactic but in doing so he was no more than ahead of his time, and he certainly did not teach this practice to either Krishna or Nitya. Moreover, there is no evidence that any of his 'boys' grew up to be homosexual; indeed most of them made happy marriages."[18]

Before closing this section about Leadbeater, I must address the question of who wrote Krishnamurti's first booklet, *At the Feet of the Master*. Several articles and pamphlets accuse Leadbeater of being the true author of this little book, which has been very successful worldwide. These accusations totally disregard the fact that Marie Russak and Balfour-Clarke both observed Krishnamurti writing the book. "Unsympathetic skeptics have often suggested and tried to prove that a boy of thirteen years of age could not write the book *At the Feet of the Master* himself. In refutation of such allegations I wish to record my personal testimony to the effect that I know that he did write it, because I saw him writing with my own eyes. It had been my proud privilege then to teach English to Krishnaji which enabled him to write down what his Master had spoken to him."[19] I regard the accounts of these witnesses as more trustworthy than the statements of people who formed their opinions based on remarks Krishnamurti himself made on the topic. *At the Feet of the Master* was written in times of awakening and the booklet remains an impressive testimony to the spiritual experiences of the young Krishnamurti.

In addition, the controversy around this book seems to have been compounded in part because the next generation of 'Krishnamurti Fans' tried to totally demystify him. However, this attempt does not consider the many mystical experiences that occurred during Krishnamurti's childhood.

Krishnamurti's mother was clairvoyant to a certain degree and she was also able to see the human aura.[20] Krishnamurti himself saw his mother several times after her early death,[21] read unopened letters, and was able to read and to see thoughts.[22] All these abilities which are documented from the time *before* he had any contact with the Theosophical Society cannot have been 'imprinted' or 'pressed upon' him—to use his words. On the other hand, these abilities did not mean much to him. He recalls in his journal: "Ever since he (Krishnamurti, P.M.) was a boy it had been like that, no thought entered his mind. He was watching and listening and nothing else."[23] Everything seems to happen through Krishnamurti rather than to him or at his own instigation. The events of that time are deeply connected to the mystery of Krishnamurti. This becomes even clearer when one considers an episode that occurred in winter 1969. During one of the rare times in which Krishnamurti spoke about his own past he touched upon this early phase in his childhood. "The boy, who was totally innocent and unaffected, still had to be protected so that evil could not touch him, could not enter him. Suddenly, in the middle of the conversation, Krishnaji stopped speaking. He said: 'We are speaking of dangerous things. It can bring it into the house.' The voice of Krishnaji was strange, his body gathered itself together. 'Can you feel it in the room?' The room was pulsating. Strong forces were alive and in movement. Krishnaji was silent for a time. When he started speaking again, the atmosphere in the room was transformed; there was silence, an active quality of goodness. Krishnaji continued."[24] These words indicate how deeply Krishnamurti's destiny was intertwined with another reality. Even as a youth

21

the beings and energies of a higher realm surrounded him, beings and energies perceptible by other people as well. "I felt a harmony that was beyond anything I had known before and it lasted throughout the period I was associated with them (Krishnamurti and his brother Nitya, P.M.)."[25]

His unusual charisma is described once more in a document written about Krishnamurti by P. G. Woodhouse in 1919, again referring to the quality of selflessness: "What struck us particularly was his naturalness...of any kind of a side or affection there was not a trace. He was still of a retiring nature, modest and deferential to his elders and courteous to all. To those whom he liked, moreover, he showed a kind of eager affection, which was singularly attractive. Of his 'occult' position he seemed to be entirely unconscious. He never alluded to it—never for a moment, allowed the slightest hint of it to get into his speech or manner.... Another quality was a serene unselfishness. He seemed to be not in the least preoccupied with himself.... We were no blind devotees, prepared to see in him nothing but perfection. We were older people, educationalists, and with some experience of youth. Had there been a trace in him of conceit or affection, or any posing as the 'holy child' or a priggish self-consciousness, we would undoubtedly have given an adverse verdict."[26]

Were the discontinuities in Krishnamurti's life, as seemingly spectacular as the dissolution of the Order of the Star, a mere shaking-off of unnecessary ballast to help that inner light shine in its true brightness, a light that was already burning in the year of his discovery? Did those beings have Leadbeater and Krishnamurti meet so he would be freed, as Pupul Jayakar reasons, from "a condition of birth and country,"[27] and so help him search for his own way, without cultural boundaries? It is surprising that Krishnamurti some-

22

times considered the question as to what would have become of him had Leadbeater not discovered him—but never searched for an answer to the question about which twist of fate had led to the events that had him *being* discovered. Perhaps he wanted other people to search for this answer, as he indicated several times in discussions with Mary Lutyens and Mary Zimbalist.

II. The Vocation

It is not clear whether Annie Besant and C. W. Leadbeater were inspired to their idea of a World Teacher by certain occult doctrines.[28] More likely, the basis for this idea can be found in their inner experiences, an hypothesis that is supported by certain remarks made by Annie Besant. Even in September 1927 when Krishnamurti was already talking about different ideas than those of the Theosophical Society, Annie Besant held true to the model that Krishnamurti was 'overshadowed' by the World Teacher. To explain her belief she points to a personal experience she had before the discovery of Krishnamurti by Leadbeater. "In 1909, the World Teacher himself had told me he had chosen a little boy and when this boy would grow up to be a man, he would use him when he will come into our world again soon."[29] This theory is supported also by the actions of both Annie Besant and C. W. Leadbeater, who in the years of preparation of Krishnamurti always stressed the last decision by the Masters. Therefore, it seems to make no sense to consider an outer source to account for the idea of the World Teacher. Even the identification of the Lord Maitreya with both Sri Krishna and Christ is more likely based on a vision of Besant and Leadbeater than on the inspiration of a third party. An objection that is sometimes raised, that the announcement of the coming of the World Teacher was only Leadbeater's concern and that Annie Besant was dependent on him in this regard, is not correct. Annie Besant herself proclaimed the coming of the World Teacher before she sacrificed her clairvoyant abilities for her engagement in the Indian fight for independence. Of all the members of the Theosophical Society, it seems that she was the only one who stood by Krishnamurti in absolute loyalty until her death, and she never doubted his mission, even though she did not fully appreciate all the steps he took or all the aspects of his teachings.[30]

Leadbeater discovered Krishnamurti in May 1909 and immediately afterwards he informed Ernest Wood that Krishnamurti would be the chosen 'vehicle' for the Lord Maitreya. However, Leadbeater did not imagine that the boy Krishnamurti would be of interest to the public so soon. He thought Krishnamurti would be educated in obscurity before taking up his duties in the world. As Leadbeater wrote in his commentary to *At the Feet of the Master*, only after a suggestion by the Maitreya did he decide to publish the little book under the pseudonym Alcyone and therefore place Krishnamurti in the public eye.[31]

The followers of the older Krishnamurti often do not consider that in his early years it was not only Krishnamurti who encountered the Masters but also that these experiences were shared by the people around him. Krishnamurti himself was in close contact with the Master Kut Humi whom he saw in his spiritual form and with whom he discussed several topics. These discussions continued until one morning he approached the materialized form of Kut Humi, walked through it—and when he turned around, the form had vanished, never to appear again.[32] One could argue that at this moment the 'Hierarchy of the Masters' ceased to exist for Krishnamurti but it will become clear that this does not hold true. It is possible that Krishnamurti interrupted a particular connection with his symbolic action but the influence of another reality did not stop after this morning.

There are a number of incidents that occurred around the time of Krishnamurti's vocation. For example, one night he put one of the first copies of *At the Feet of the Master* under his pillow. R. Balfour-Clarke closed the mosquito net around the bed in a way that Krishnamurti would not have been able to duplicate from within the net. At 5 am Balfour-Clarke woke Krishnamurti, opened the mosquito net, and together they realized that the little blue book had vanished. One thought that Kut Humi had taken it.[33]

More impressive than this 'occult episode' are the mystical experiences of those people who met the young Krishnamurti. The encounter with an enormous, unknown energy which for many of those people was quite frightening, left all of them with a deep spiritual impression. Emily Lutyens, Krishnamurti's most important motherly mentor after Annie Besant, wrote about one of those events: "It is very difficult to convey the extraordinary and marvelous atmosphere of those evenings. Although I am not in the least psychic, I felt very strongly the presence of the Masters, and was not at all surprised when Krishna told us that on several occasions the Lord Maitreya himself had been there. The atmosphere began to change after 3 pm. It was as if it were charged with some terrific force, increasing in intensity up til the end of his meditation which lasted for about an hour, and then dying away, leaving behind it a wonderful sense of peace."[34] I certainly do not believe in some form of theosophical mass hysteria to which all of these people had succumbed and which made them experience visions that are in harmony with a theosophical world view, and I will present documentation later which supports my point of view. These experiences, in the vicinity of the young Krishnamurti, were both deeply moving and of undoubted honesty. However, unanswered questions still remain about the meaning of these incidents and how it was even possible for them to occur—for example, through the presence of the Masters, etc. I attempt to answer these questions in Chapter IV.

After entering the Theosophical Society, the first important 'esoteric' step in Krishnamurti's life happened on January 10, 1910. The astrological constellations for this day were considered excellent from a theosophical point of view. However, Leadbeater thought it was still too early for Krishnamurti's first initiation because he had only five months of apprenticeship. It seems strange to me that nobody seemed to have considered that Krishnamurti had already taken the first steps of the initiation in an earlier life. However, a few days before January 10, Leadbeater received an order from the Master, and for thirty-six hours he secluded Krishnamurti and himself in Annie Besant's rooms. The experiences of those dramatic hours are very well documented.[35] It is not clear whether the reports by Leadbeater and Krishnamurti were a shared illusion, a projection made by Leadbeater on Krishnamurti—who was easily influenced, or true transformations. Later, Krishnamurti did not remember these events of January 1910. Both Leadbeater and Besant had no doubt that the events were real.[36] It is impossible to find an answer that is above all suspicion but the photographs of Krishnamurti taken after his return to the real world following those hours of seclusion remain intact. I do not recall ever seeing a photograph of a human being of similar beauty and spiritual emanation as that taken of the young Krishnamurti on the day of his presumed initiation.[37] Whatever really happened during those thirty-six

28

hours in January 1910, an encounter with a higher reality must have occurred. Otherwise, the transformation of the unprepossessing Hindu boy into that figure of transfigured glory cannot be understood.

In this connection, I draw your attention to a seemingly unimportant episode of October 1984, the evening before the murder of Indira Gandhi. Pupul Jayakar had already finished most of her biography on Krishnamurti and he was staying in her house that night. Krishnamurti asked her to read to him from her book. Mary Zimbalist, who was also staying with them, read parts about his birth and childhood to him. Then Pupul Jayakar continued reading. Later, she wrote about the events that followed: "Krishnaji had been totally still during the reading. He only interrupted once when he heard me read the passage on Alcyone, in which I had said that the word Alcyone meant 'kingfisher,' the calmer of the storms. He interrupted to correct me. 'No,' he said, 'it means 'the brightest star in the Pleiades.'" As the reading continued, the feeling of presence was overpowering, and soon my voice stopped. Krishnaji turned to me, 'Do you feel It? I could prostrate to It?' His body was trembling as he spoke of the presence that listened. 'Yes, I can prostrate to this, that is here.' Suddenly he turned and left us walking alone to his room."[38] What kind of being manifested itself in that room and what was the connection to the events of the life of the young Krishnamurti? Was a circle closed here, just fifteen months before Krishnamurti's death? Did the energy, the being that had accompanied and inspired Krishnamurti and had looked after him all his life manifest itself? I believe that both the young and the old Krishnamurti had been particularly close to the enlightened beings of a higher reality. In any case, this event is remarkable because it hints of a Krishnamurti who was touched deeply within, even though in his talks he consistently rejected any form of religious devotion. Even—or especially?—a radical free-thinker like Krishnamurti bows down before the presence of the Holy.

One might anticipate that Krishnamurti was quite happy in his 'pre-messiah' time but this only holds true for the early years. By 1914 he had already written and spoken to Emily Lutyens about his dissatisfaction with his destiny.[39] During that period he was more interested in playing golf, enjoying his new motorcycle, or in other amusements.[40] For the ascetic-esoteric-raised Krishnamurti, problems brought on by puberty seem not to have arisen until somewhat later and perhaps only in his dreams, of which he wrote to Emily Lutyens.[41] In the case of a 'normal' person it might be appropriate to search for known psychological patterns or for a suppressed sexual neurosis but I believe those methods to be of no help in Krishnamurti's case. One must always consider that Krishnamurti is not at all a 'normal' person. At times isolated, 'normal' problem structures did occur, but they dissolved after a brief period and were supplanted and raised by more important transformations of consciousness.

The years between 1910 and 1920 were times of severe emotional fluctuation for Krishnamurti, both in personal matters as well as in his spiritual mission. Those days in 1920 that he spent in Paris with a close family, the Manziarlys, exemplify this. On the one hand he expressed his doubts about what Besant and Leadbeater had said. On the other hand he was confronted by his own deeply mystical experiences, which were even recognized by those around him. However, he did not reach an inner clarity.[42]

It was not until 1922 that he seemed to have re-established a stronger connection to the world of the Masters. In a letter to Emily Lutyens he wrote: "I feel once again in touch with Lord Maitreya and the Masters and there is nothing else for me to do but to serve Them."[43] A change seems to have occurred, his role as the Messiah of theosophical form transformed to a World Teacher in his own right.

30

III. Messiah or World Teacher

On January 11, 1911, the *Order of the Rising Sun* was founded on the initiative of George Arundale. This organization was meant to gather those people who were waiting for the coming of a new great teacher. A few months later, Annie Besant took over this organization, changed its name to the *Order of the Star in the East*, and asked Krishnamurti to become its head. To become a member of the Order, it was sufficient to sign a piece of paper stating six central ideas:

1. The belief in the coming of a great teacher and the wish to lead a life of preparation for this event.

2. To keep the coming of the great teacher ever in one's consciousness and to live accordingly.

3. To dedicate a part of one's daily activities to the coming.

4. To develop devotion, steadfastness, and kindness.

5. To begin and end each day with a plea for *His* blessing.

6. To strive for cooperation with those who one recognizes as spiritual leaders.[44]

With the Order of the Star, an instrument had been created to provide a body for the new teacher. It was a time of messianic expectation; but the expectation would continue for fourteen more years until the first public manifestation of the connection of Krishnamurti with the Lord Maitreya occurred. On December 28, 1925, in Adyar, Krishnamurti gave a talk during a gathering of the Order of the Star. During his talk, his voice suddenly changed and he started to use the first person instead of the third. Before that moment he had spoken about the coming of the World Teacher and now, for the first time, he said: "I am coming."[45] From that moment on, the Theosophists and the members of the Order of the Star believed that the coming had begun. Annie Besant recalled a discussion between herself and Krishnamurti immediately after the event: "Then, Krishnaji went to his seat. I asked him later, whether or not he knew what he had said, he answered, 'No.' I asked him, what he felt; he said he felt like he had just woken up from a dream; that he was still dizzy. And this is an accurate description of what really had happened."[46] Unfortunately, Krishnamurti was later unable to clarify these events. He also seems to have had unanswered questions.

The most informative comments about the events of the twenties can be found in the books by Geoffrey Hodson. Hodson was a young theosophist then, with what seems to have been a remarkable clairvoyance. Taking into account his pure life over the following sixty years—he died in 1983— his testimony deserves high regard. During several talks with his biographer Kirk Robertson,[47] Hodson stressed the 'experimental character' of what can be best described as the 'over-shadowing' of Krishnamurti by the Lord Maitreya. Hodson's description of the events during the meeting of the Order of the Star in August 1927 in Ommen provide an impressive insight: "As he (Krishnamurti, P.M.) speaks, the spirit of the Christ descends, as a great ring-shaped cloud of golden light. It hovers over our heads, descends still lower, slowly and gently, like a warm summer rain, till all are enwrapped in its beauty, its peace and all-compelling love.

"The voice is silent.

"Night after night, as he ceases to speak, a miracle occurs. Two thousand seven hundred people remain perfectly still. In that silence the splendor of splendors is revealed to the inner eyes. The figure of the Lord appears above the head of Krishnaji. The silence deepens. We are enfolded in His embrace, filled with tenderness and compassion as He draws near."[48] Hodson regarded those events as 'unforgettable;' he considered them the highlight of his spiritual experiences. He wrote about several of his remembrances and sensations in a manuscript called *The Unforgettable Years*, but he did not publish it. Even the publication of his diaries, edited by his wife after his death, do not refer to those years.[48a]

During a talk with Robertson, Hodson stated his opinion that the Masters had a definite plan in this 'experiment' involving the overshadowing of Krishnamurti, and the role of C. W. Leadbeater had only been to publicly proclaim what he had been told by the Masters. Hodson believed the reason for its failure—in a way—had several aspects. In his opinion, the two main reasons were Krishnamurti's withdrawal into himself, brought on by an inner (emotional) injury based on several unpleasant events within the Theosophical Society, and an unbearable nervous strain. Hodson referred to a statement by Krishnamurti's physician at that time who had told him that the nervous and emotional pressure brought upon Krishnamurti would be enormous, even if his body was taken over by that higher being for only a few minutes.[49] When the Theosophists realized that the overshadowing was not going to happen as they had imagined, they began to emphasize the *differences* between Krishnamurti and the World Teacher. For example, Leadbeater wrote in a letter to Annie Besant: "Of course our Krishnaji has not the Omniscience of the Lord. No physical body of our stage could, I imagine, have that, I say so quite frankly."[50] The paradox is that Krishnamurti regarded himself more as a World Teacher later—in his own right—

than the Theosophists, whose messianic ideal he had rejected inwardly and outwardly for several years, ever did. However, before we continue with Krishnamurti's own experiences, the testimonies of other people, who were sitting at the feet of Krishnamurti throughout those years, should also be considered.

While the reports of moving, overwhelming experiences in the presence of Krishnamurti are countless, three special events stand out. The first, when Krishnamurti handed over the membership certificates for the Order of the Star in December, 1911 in Benares; the second, the 'great experience' in the second half of August 1922, and the third—the first overshadowing—occurred again on a 28th of December but this time in 1925 and in Adyar. There are dramatic reports by eyewitnesses to all of these events.

On April 11, 1912, Leadbeater published an article titled *A Momentous Incident* in the *Herald of the Star*. Leadbeater reported the events of the 28th of December, 1911. For example, he wrote: "All at once the Hall was filled with a tremendous power, which was so evidently flowing through Alcyone (Krishnamurti, P.M.) that the next member fell at his feet, overwhelmed by this marvelous rush of force. I have never seen or felt anything in the least like it; it reminded one irresistibly of the rushing, mighty wind, and the outpouring of the Holy Ghost at Pentecost. The tension was enormous, and everyone in the room was most powerfully affected. It was exactly the kind of things that we read about in the old scriptures, and think exaggerated; but here it was before us in the twentieth century... I have seen many things in occultism, but never on the physical plane such an outpouring of force as this, nor anything, which moved all present so profoundly."[51] There are several other eyewitness reports of this event but the most convincing one seems to be by Major C. L. Peacocke,[52] which includes a characterization of the people attending the meeting, who ranged from high-ranking British military officers and university professors to simple people, all of them having been overwhelmed by the divine Power. In particular, Peacocke points out, it would have been totally impossible for high-ranking officers and professors to bow before a Hindu boy had they not been deeply moved—remember these events occurred in 1911.

During Krishnamurti's 'Great Experience' in the summer of 1922, only three other people were present: Krishnamurti's brother, Nitya, A. P. Warrington, and Rosalind Williams. In a moving letter dated August 17, 1922, Nitya wrote about the dramatic events to A. Besant and C. W. Leadbeater. Krishnamurti had gone through a long transformation process. One evening, he was meditating beneath a young pepper tree in Ojai while Rosalind, Nitya, and Warrington observed him from a distance a few steps away. Then the following happened: "The place seemed to be filled with a Great Presence and a great longing came upon me to go on my knees and adore, for I knew that the Great Lord of all our hearts had come Himself; and though we saw Him not, yet all felt the splendor of His presence. Then the eyes of Rosalind were opened and she saw. Her face changed as I have seen no face change, for she was blessed enough to see with physical eyes the glories of that night. Her face was transfigured, as she said to us, 'Do you see Him, do you see Him?' For she saw the divine Bodhisattva (The Lord Maitreya) and millions wait for incarnations to catch such a glimpse of our Lord, but she had eyes of innocence and had served our Lord faithfully and we who could not see saw the Splendors of the night mirrored in her face pale with the rapture in the starlight. Never shall I forget the look on her face, for presently I who could not see but who gloried in the presence of our Lord felt that He turned towards us and spoke some words to Rosalind; her face shone with divine ecstasy as she answered, 'I will, I will,' and she spoke the words as if they were a promise given with splendid joy. Never shall I forget her face when I looked at her; even I was almost blessed with a vision. Her face showed the rapture of her heart, for the innermost part of her being was ablaze with His presence but her eyes saw...."[53] These events were so sacred to those present that they were only made public after several years. From that moment on, Krishnamurti had an even more intense charisma.

I have already commented on Krishnamurti's first public overshadowing in December, 1925, with the description provided by G. Hodson. I add the report of one eyewitness, who observed the events amongst the public attendees and who did not have a significant role in the Theosophical Society of those times. It is the report by a Dutch woman called Dijkgraf. She wrote: "Suddenly I knew that the words I heard were those of the Master. I cannot express this in words, but felt it as a holy presence in my heart, which filled the whole atmosphere and eliminated all that was unreal. For a single moment my whole universe stood still.... I looked up into the calm of Krishnamurti's face. I saw no physical change, but never before had I seen such love of mankind shine from a person's eyes."[54]

Those reports, written by three totally different personalities and referring in part to other eyewitnesses, are impressive accounts of the immense spiritual powers that influenced Krishnamurti during this 'messianic period.' It is just not possible to explain all of these accounts as occurrences of blindness or self-deception. The influence of a higher reality was too intense. Notwithstanding the changes that occurred in the Krishnamurti of the years after 1930, during the first thirty to thirty-five years of his life, there was a sphere of holiness in him, through him, and around him, a world of divine beings revealed. Revelations occurred which transformed everybody entering the force-field of the young Krishnamurti.

There can be no doubt that Krishnamurti himself was moved deeply by the emanating energy. After the events of August, 1922, he wrote to C. W. Leadbeater: "I feel once again in touch with Lord Maitreya and the Master and there is nothing else for me to do but to serve Them. My whole life, now, is consciously, on the physical plane, devoted to the work and I am not likely to change."[55] At the same time he expresses himself in a poetic way: "Nothing could ever be the same. I have drunk of the clear pure waters at the source of the fountain of life and my soul was appeased. Never more could I be thirsty, never more could I be in utter darkness. I have seen the Light. I have touched compassion which heals all sorrow and suffering; it is not for myself, but for the world. I have stood on the mountain top and gazed at the mighty Beings. Never can I be in utter darkness; I have seen the glorious and healing Light. The fountain Truth has been revealed to me and the darkness has been dispersed. Love in all its glory has intoxicated my heart; my heart can never be closed. I have drunk at the fountain of joy and eternal Beauty. I am God-intoxicated!"[56] All events and spiritual processes seem to confirm Leadbeater's forecasts. The events indicated that there was every reason to regard Krishnamurti as a tool for the Maitreya or for another high being. However, things were to develop differently.

Between 1925 and 1927 a change appeared in Krishnamurti that led him away from his pre-defined role as Messiah and to a new form of how he saw himself as a World Teacher. Annie Besant's premonition was accurate when she described Krishnamurti during a talk in 1927 as follows: "He talks with great dignity and authority. He takes a standpoint as never before. He always was reluctant to be used by the World Teacher, because he was very shy; now he said, he is the World Teacher and is teaching.—That's where things are right now. If you ask me, how he changed, I can only tell you that I have watched him over the last months. It seems to be less a taking possession of the body, as it was in 1925, and more of a successive process of melting of consciousness with parts of the consciousness of the World Teacher, as far as this can express itself through the human body."[57] During several interviews when he was questioned about his role as Messiah, Krishnamurti tried to find an interpretation of his task and of the way he saw himself as World Teacher. In his remarkable talk during the summer camp in Eerde in 1927, he spoke of himself as a World Teacher for the first time: "I never said: I am the World Teacher; but now that I feel that I am one with my Beloved, I say it, not in order to impress my authority on you, not to convince you of my greatness, nor of the greatness of the World Teacher, nor even of the beauty of life, but merely to awaken the desire in your hearts and in your minds to seek out the Truth. If I say, and I will say, that I am one with my Beloved, it is because I feel and know it. I have found what I longed for, I have become united, so that hence for there will be no separation, because my thoughts, my desires, my longings—those of the individual self, have been destroyed.... I am as the flower that gives scent to the morning air. It does not concern itself with who is passing by.... Until now you have been depending on the two Protectors of the Order (Mrs. Besant and Leadbeater) for authority, on

38

someone else to tell you the Truth, whereas the Truth lies within you…. It is no good asking me who is the Beloved. Of what use is the explanation? For you will not understand the Beloved until you are able to see him in every animal, every blade of grass, in every person that is suffering, in every individual."[58]

In a conversation after the camp in Eerde, he gave a definition of the term World Teacher which is truly characteristic of both his modesty and his humor: "It is very simple. The World Teacher is one who goes round the world teaching."[59] Becoming more serious, he closed the conversation with a deeper definition: "I hold that there is an eternal Life which is the Source and the Goal, the beginning and the end and yet it is without end or beginning. In that Life alone is there fulfillment. And any one that fulfills that Life has the key to the Truth without limitation. That Life is for all. Into that Life the Buddha, the Christ have entered. From my point of view, I have attained, I have entered into that Life. That Life has no form, as Truth has no form, no limitation. And to that Life everyone must return."[60] During the following two years, as Krishnamurti moved even further from his earlier role as Messiah, he tried to shift the traditional background, the theosophical or classical traditional cosmos, to an impersonal absolute. Two interviews from those years give an impression of that attitude. In 1928, he gave the answer to a questioner in London: "Sir, I have said over and over again that, according to me, Krishnamurti as such no longer exists. As the river enters the sea and loses itself in the sea, so Krishnamurti has entered into that Life which is represented by some as the Christ, by others as The Buddha, by others still, as the Lord Maitreya. Hence Krishnamurti as an entity fully developed has entered into the Sea of Life and is the Teacher, because the moment you enter into that Life—which is the fulfillment of all Teachers, which is life of all the Teachers—the individual as such ceases."[61] Krishnamurti tried to begin a new way of communicating his inner experiences without using an old framework or paying tribute to old ways of thinking. More and more, the traditional religious ways seemed to become boundaries instead of tools on the way to the 'pathless land.' In spring 1929 he was interviewed by the American journalist Gladys Baker for the *Birmingham New-Age Herald*. The April 1, 1929, edition of the *Herald* states: "'As far as I am concerned, Krishnamurti, as such, has ceased to exist,' he began frankly. 'He has entered into that life which is represented to some as the Christ, to others as the Buddha and to those in the East as Shri Krishna. In the plan we have been discussing there must exist the principle of brotherhood. The teachers of all ages have repeated the same essentials but we never seem to understand them, perhaps because of their very simplicity. And so,' he went on, 'when it becomes necessary for humanity to receive in a new form the ancient wisdom someone whose duty it is to repeat these truths is incarnated.'"[62] For somebody carefully observing Krishnamurti after 1926, reading about the talks and interviews he gave, it was clear that a deep transformation was gradually taking place. The differences between his inner goal and the concepts into which the Theosophical Society, particularly Arundale and Wedgwood, tried to press him, became too pronounced. The events moved on to a climax that was to mark a radical cut.

IV. The Renunciation

In my view, 1925 must be regarded as the key year for the inner development of Krishnamurti. I try to explain my reasons for this opinion in the following.

In the summer of that year the fraction centered around Arundale and Wedgwood assembled in the Dutch Huizen; later, Annie Besant, Emily Lutyens, and other prominent theosophists arrived. What happened then can only be described as pseudo-esoteric hysteria. In weeks, sometimes only days, normal people evolved to the level of initiates and mahatmas. In just a few weeks Rukmini Arundale had climbed to the level of a master, with three initiations in as many days. Unfortunately, Besant no longer had the strength to recognize these illusions as such and to stop them. Leadbeater sent an angry rebuttal after he learned about these events. Leadbeater's annoyance about the 'nonsense of Huizen' must have been expressed very bluntly, as Dora Kunz, then one of his closest collaborators, told me in a private conversation. Only his loyalty to Besant prevented him from making his opinion public.

This kind of initiation hysteria, combined with the self-nomination of his apostles, had a devastating effect on Krishnamurti. He was deeply hurt by the desecration of names and spirit-filled acts that were deeply sacred to him. Two reports give evidence for Krishnamurti's inner crisis that was triggered by the events in Huizen. In London, he met Emily Lutyens again and with resignation he told her about his feelings: "She (Lady Emily) found him 'terribly unhappy about the whole affair, disbelieving everything.'

He felt that something infinitely precious, sacred and private had been made public, ugly and ridiculous, cheap and vulgar. Lady Emily asked him why he did not say openly what he felt, to which he replied. 'What would be the use?' They would only say that the Black Powers had got hold of him. However he did try several times to talk to Mrs. Besant, but, according to Lady Emily, she did not seem to take it in; it was almost as if she had been hypnotized by George (Arundale)."[63] The 'Black Powers' referred to an intrigue of Wedgwood who attempted to get Annie Besant to believe all (in his view) critical remarks by Krishnamurti were inspired by a well-known black magician—a slandering that hurt Krishnamurti deeply. How badly he was treated by Wedgwood and Arundale can only be surmised through the reports of contemporary witnesses because Krishnamurti himself did not talk about it in public, due to his natural politeness and his consideration for Besant. However, in his diaries Sidney Field recalls conversations from those times when Krishnamurti expressed clear indignation.[64]

The most impressive evidence about Krishnamurti's feelings is a letter he wrote—interestingly enough—to Leadbeater. It says: "Wedgwood is distributing initiations around.... Initiations and sacred things will be a joke presently.... I believe in all this so completely that it makes me weep to see these sacred things dragged in the dirt."[65] For one who has developed an understanding of Krishnamurti's emotional vulnerability, those lines are exceptionally meaningful. This is one of the key factors in his breaking-up with his theosophical past—the second factor would be even more painful.

In February 1925, Krishnamurti wrote about a dream in a letter to Annie Besant. He had been with the Masters to ask that Nitya recover from his illness. The Lord Maitreya had listened to him and had answered: "He will be well." Krishnamurti wrote to Annie Besant about how relieved and happy he had been when he received this promise.[66] Due to his unbounded belief in the Masters, Krishnamurti was absolutely sure now that his brother, who was suffering from tuberculosis, would be healed. On November 13, 1925, on a stormy night and as Krishnamurti crossed the Suez Canal, he received a telex with the message of Nitya's death. According to the reports of Krishnamurti's companions on this journey, the news left him totally broken. I am convinced that his world view collapsed that night. If one is looking for the key to Krishnamurti's radical rejection of the esoteric world view, this, in my view, is it. At that moment, Krishnamurti must have come to the extremely painful realization that the esoteric teachings had let him down—at least the teachings as he understood them. One must read his 1931 reflection on Nitya's death very carefully to sense his amazing naiveté on the one hand, and what I would call an escape into the unity of the Absolute on the other. "When my brother was ill, I used to keep awake at night, looking at the stars making their way across the horizon and wondering if they could save his life. I watched the shade of every tree in the daytime, questioning it, whether it could protect him. But it did not protect. And I saw that life is one, though it has many expressions, that as long as I separated myself from my brother, from that life which was in him, I longed for fleeting comfort, fleeting shadows of understanding, I prayed and questioned every passer-by. But the moment I realized that, whenever there is life, it is one, though there may be a multitude of expressions of that life, I ceased to grieve."[67] This mysticism of unity, which helped him to overcome the pain and the loneliness of death, even moved the perception of his deceased brother into the background.

"I have seen my brother. Now I know. I have seen him as happy as a bird in the blue skies, for it is a tremendous relief for him to be released from that body."[68]

Only a few days after Nitya's death and while still on his journey to Colombo, Krishnamurti's inner transformation took place. As a result, it was a stronger and quite different Krishnamurti who faced his audience in Adyar and, as mentioned earlier, who spoke in the first person for the first time. This 'revelation' and Nitya's death might be more closely related than has been acknowledged in the past. Nitya's death opened a door for the experience of a unity that was connected to radical freedom and to total detachment.

Nitya's death was a dramatic break; the process of ripening in the years before and after are only the prelude and epilogue to the real act of renunciation, the dissolution of the Order of the Star. By the early twenties, Krishnamurti had already rejected his role as Messiah[69] and, from 1927 on, his rejection was manifested to the outside world. Emily Lutyens made a note about Krishnamurti's words in July, 1927, in Eerde: "You must not make me an authority. If I become a necessity to you what will you do when I go away?....Some of you think I can give you a drink that will set you free, that I can give you a formula that will liberate you—that is not so. I can be the door but you must pass through the door and find the liberation that is beyond it."[70] One year later, his words were even clearer: "Do not quote me afterwards as an authority. I refuse to be your crutch. I am not going to be brought into a cage for your worship."[71] In those two quotes, Krishnamurti set a basic tone that he would maintain until the end of his life. In 1925, during his last talks in Saanen, he continued his clarification in his third talk: "I am *not* your leader, I am *not* your helper, I am *not* your guru—thank God! We are together, as two brothers, and I mean it, the speaker *means* it, it is not just words."[72] Despite the withdrawal of his *person*, he never had any doubt about his *task* and his authorization as a teacher. In May 1929, a few months before he dissolved the Order of the Star in Ommen, he stated very clearly: "I say now, I say without conceit, with proper understanding, with fullness of mind and heart, that I am that full flame which is the glory of life, to which all human beings, individuals as well as the whole world, must come."[73] Like countless other similar statements he has made, these sentences exemplify the peculiar tension between the human being Krishnamurti, with his radical rejection of the guru role, and the emphasis he placed on the importance of the teachings. This tendency continued for his entire life—I might even call it an anxious concern he had about the purity of the teachings. This concern is in a peculiar contrast to his otherwise spiritual sovereignty.

On the morning of August 3, 1929, Krishnamurti ended a memorable period of his life—he dissolved the Order of the Star in the East. His remarkable talk has been both cited and published many times in the past and so I will restrict myself to only a few prominent passages. "Truth, being limitless, unconditioned, unapproachable by any path whatsoever, cannot be organized; nor should any organization be formed to lead or coerce people along any particular path. If you first understand that, then you will see how impossible it is to organize a belief. A belief is purely an individual matter, and you cannot and must not organize it. If you do it, it becomes dead, crystallized; it becomes a creed, a sect, a religion, to be imposed on others....

"Again, you have the idea that only certain people hold the key to the Kingdom of Happiness. No one holds it. No one has the authority to hold that key. That key is your own self and in the development and the purification and in the incorruptibility of that self alone is the Kingdom of Eternity....

"My only concern is to set men absolutely, unconditionally free."[74]

The dissolution of the Order of the Star and his renunciation of his role as Messiah, which he did not find appropriate for himself, are acts of greatness that one does not find often in the field of religion. These acts shine like a crystal-clear symbol over Krishnamurti; they stand for truthfulness, honesty, and purity. Only a soul that had truly overcome would be able to manifest the power to cut all connections to the past—including the conveniences associated with them—and to embark upon new paths, being both free and living from the source of life itself.

V. The Transformation

After the dissolution of the Order of the Star, Krishnamurti's life goal and philosophy did not change over night. Rather, the inner liberation was simply documented by an outer act. At a meeting in Ommen in 1927, Krishnamurti had already hinted at his intent that the rejection of all authority would move into the focal point of his teachings. "Suppose a certain person was able to tell you that I am the World Teacher, in what way would it help, in what way would it alter the Truth? In what way would understanding come to your heart, and knowledge come to your mind? If you depend on authority, you will be building your foundations on the sands, and the wave of sorrow will come and wash them away. But if you build your foundations in stone, the stone of your own experience of your own knowledge, of your own sorrows and your own sufferings, if you are able to build your house on that, brick by brick, experience upon experience, then you will be able to convince others."[75] For the first time, his conflict with the Theosophical Society reached a point where the irreconcilable differences became apparent. Krishnamurti rejected the Masters, the path of initiation, in brief everything having to do with theosophical esoteric, as unimportant. In doing so he sometimes used rather sarcastic words. For example, in Eerde he answered a question addressed to him with: "I don't know what the theosophical divine plan is."[76] Since he had lived with Annie Besant and C. W. Leadbeater for more than twenty years, the polemic nature of this sentence was quite clear, above its rhetoric, educational implication.

The times following the dissolution of the Order of the Star and the deaths of both Besant and Leadbeater—from September, 1933 to March, 1934—were overshadowed by a heavy tension between Krishnamurti and the Theosophical Society. The climax was reached when Krishnamurti was thrown off the grounds of the Theosophical Society in Adyar just after Arundale was elected President of the Society. At that time, Krishnamurti referred to theosophical circles only as 'the Gang.' Unfortunately, his words were not chosen with great consideration either, such as the time he called the leaders of the Theosophical Society 'exploiters.' This controversy became so harsh that an ever-mild Geoffrey Hodson felt the urge to write a polemic against Krishnamurti. He arrives at the conclusion: "Since, however, I have long admired and respected Krishnamurti, I give serious consideration to his accusations. I give particular attention to his use of the word 'exploiters' in connection with such people as Madame Blavatsky, Colonel Olcott, Dr. Besant, C. W. Leadbeater and their successors. I have looked at these people with unbiased eyes. I have watched closely for any sign whatever of self-seeking and 'exploitation' in the conduct of their lives and in their relations with their fellow men, especially with those who have felt most intimately drawn to them. Dispassionately and with every opportunity of knowing the facts, with Krishnamurti's arraignment before me, I have presumed to judge The Theosophical Society, its founders, its leaders and all those tens of thousands who love and serve under them. I give my verdict unhesitatingly.

"It is: 'Not Guilty.'"[77]

Krishnamurti did not want to step down from his lofty mountain peak, a point I discuss in more detail in Chapter XII on 'Evolution.' He refused to give crutches to those who were searching for a path. This was a point where Annie Besant had a different opinion. She regarded it as her duty to provide a crutch for the feeble and so help them move forward, even if only a little. Unfortunately, any substantive discussion was lost in the polemic about the Masters. Many years later, this is further clarified in a sentence by Mary Lutyens who describes the situation in the early thirties: "If the Masters were no longer recognized, Leadbeater, as their chief lieutenant, would lose all his power and prestige."[78] It is difficult for me to understand how someone who knew Leadbeater very well could reduce his spiritual authorization to the 'chief lieutenant' of the Masters. Leadbeater's main books on esoteric topics, e.g., *The Inner Life, Forms of Thought,* or *Chakras* to name only a few, influenced generations and contributed substantially to the building of a new understanding of the world and of mankind. Limiting his role to that of an emissary between pupil and Master completely overlooks his real importance in this process.

It is noteworthy that during the last years of his life Krishnamurti again developed a sense for the original intentions of the Theosophical Society and its leaders. An event from the year 1981 documents this: "Krishnaji's mood was changing, he was speaking from great depth, as if traveling swiftly vast spaces within. 'I think there is a force which the Theosophists had touched but tried to make into something concrete. There was something they had touched and then tried to translate into their symbols and vocabulary, and so lost it. This feeling has been going all through my life—it is not....'

"'Linked with consciousness?' asked Achyut.

"'No, no. When I talk about it, something tremendous is going on. I can't ask it anything,' said Krishnaji.

"Through windows, doors, silence poured."[79]

During the years of Krishnamurti's transformation from theosophical messiah to a teacher in his own right, the issue was not as much to understand each role but rather to dissociate the roles. It was through this process that Krishnamurti drew more radical lines. Tolerance for each other was to be found only rarely in those days: "There's distinct antagonism but one calls that tolerance, a creation of the intellect, a cursed thing by itself."[80] G. Hodson regarded this position of Krishnamurti as a very biased and unwarranted rejection of the ways and methods of other people—a criticism which Krishnamurti faced quite frequently, especially from people who were well-meaning towards him. "Is it possible for a great reformer as Krishnamurti to display tolerance? May it not be necessary for him to be so one-pointed in the inculcation and practice of the particular aspect of truth and particular method of self-illumination which he promulgates, that he denies the existence and validity of every other aspect and every other method?"[81] The justification for this critical questioning is based on the insight that during Krishnamurti's transformation many people were left behind.[82] Many of his companions, including close friends like Emily Lutyens, simply did not understand him any longer. Their familiar cosmos had been shattered under Krishnamurti's blows and they were unable to view the new heaven from which he addressed them. This created much suffering, suffering which might have been prevented by a certain caution. As I was told in several conversations with some of those closest to Krishnamurti, in the last few years of his life, he asked himself the same question over and over again: why it was that after so many years nobody close to him had completed the 'transformation.'[83] Were his teachings too abstract?[84] Was the gap between mountain top and valley too wide? Perhaps the notion of time—of evolution—is more important than Krishnamurti was willing to admit. This conjecture is made more likely because in later years he often referred to his own process of ripening. "I can never be finished but I want to finish with all the superficialities which I have."[85] Time and again one finds sentences full of claims to absolute right. For example, in 1932 in Ojai, Krishnamurti wrote: "I have revolutionized myself! I can't tell you, mum (Emily Lutyens, P.M.), what a glorious thing it is to have realized the highest and the most sublime thing."[86]

Referring to a common polarity, his contradiction between theory—Krishnamurti's talks and discussions—and practice—Krishnamurti's personal experiences—is characteristic of his periods of transformation. It remained predominant for many years to come.

VI. New Paths

Over the years, the arguments between Krishnamurti and the Theosophical Society lessened and then finally moved completely into the background. When Krishnamurti's life-long friend Jinarajadasa died in 1953, his last point of contact with the Society was lost. Therefore, before I continue with the new paths, I will try to present a provisional summary to this point. In 1934, Krishnamurti spoke before a group of Theosophists. He was asked his opinion whether the Theosophical Society had lost its importance or whether it still had a role to play in the world. His answer, one of the most remarkable statements ever made regarding the Theosophical Society, goes far beyond the question itself. "I wonder how many of you have really asked why you belong to it. If you really are a social body, not a religious body, not an ethical body, then there is some hope for it in the world. If you are really a body of people who are discovering, not who have found, if you are a body of people who are giving information, not giving spiritual distinctions, if you are a body of people who have a really open platform, not for me or for someone special, if you are a body of people among whom there are neither leaders nor followers, then there is some hope.... Don't you see if you really thought about these things and were honest, you could be an extraordinarily useful body in the world."[87] The substantive aspects of the controversy between Krishnamurti and the Theosophical Society, which are beyond the scope of this book, are documented clearly in the 'polemic' by Geoffrey Hodson.

First, Hodson refers to Krishnamurti's thesis that everybody should be able to find inner fulfillment and self-realization spontaneously and completely, be he a 'trash collector or a university professor,' independent of his level of evolution and independent of whether he is primitive or a genius.

"'Why do they not do so?' I naturally asked.

"'Because they don't want to,' was the reply.

"'Why do they not want to?' I asked.

"'Because they have not had enough experience.'

"'Then experience has a value?'"

In Hodson's view, Krishnamurti's rejection of the idea of maturation and the significance of his inner experience had lead him to a dead end. However, according to Krishnamurti this phase was only the beginning. This becomes clearer in another statement. "Here are his (Krishnamurti's, P.M.) words on the subject: 'When we understand profoundly the significance of our existence, of the process of ignorance and action, we will see what we call purpose has no significance. The mere search for the purpose of life covers up, detracts from the comprehension of oneself.'

"That quotation is a perfect example of the closed circle of thought outside of which I for one continually find myself to be shut when endeavoring to comprehend these teachings. For the opening clause, 'When we understand profoundly the significance of our existence,' is for me the end, not the beginning of the search.

"This phenomena is constant throughout all Krishnamurti's expositions. He seems to me to put the very goal itself as the first step towards its attainment. If I may presume to say so, of one so much greater than myself, he does not appear to appreciate the enormous gulf between himself as a very great and illuminated being and the rest of humanity in which he appears to be trying to initiate the process of thinking for itself."

Then he discusses the problem of understanding and the significance of the Masters. Hodson explains: "Here, for example is a question put to him in various forms more than once: 'I have listened to your talks for several years, but to be frank, I have not yet grasped what you are trying to convey.' The answer, as usual, is itself as unacceptable (to me!) as the teachings which produce the question. Krishnamurti says: 'All that I am trying to do is to help you to discern for yourself that there is no salvation outside of yourself, that no Master, no society can save you.' Obviously that is not all he is trying to tell us; for such a statement is to be found in every one of the world religions and philosophies, and especially is it part of the central message of the one society which Krishnamurti has singled out as the chief target for his arrows of criticism and iconoclasm—The Theosophical Society."

In conclusion, I mention one other aspect of Hodson's work which I regard as very important because it shows two different attempts: "If one understands Krishnamurti rightly, he insists on bringing this condition about by force, artificially as it were. There must be a positive action to eject all previous concepts of life. 'When we begin to free ourselves, through experiment, from these false divisions...then we shall release creative energy and discover the endless movement of life.'

"My own idea of this self-clarification is that it is entirely a natural process; it is the result of interior changes, of the unfoldment of the life within. It is, therefore, not forced. Indeed, it seems doubtful whether it can be brought about artificially."[88] It may be helpful to keep this particular debate in mind when dealing with the Krishnamurti of the years that followed World War II.

The late thirties were shaped by a phase of new emergence and new beginnings. For the most part, the old ties were broken, and new ones were to be formed. Slowly, new companions emerged, but it was only after The War that an outwardly visible and effective new period in Krishnamurti's life began.

Krishnamurti spent most of the War years in seclusion in California, where his visa was extended repeatedly, despite his clearly pacifistic point of view. A conversation from the year 1949 between Krishnamurti and Dr. Adikaram illuminates his thoughts regarding the outer form of his teachings during this period. "We had stopped. As we began to walk again, Krishnaji asked, 'What is the Sanskrit word for 'awareness'?

"Adikaram pondered a moment. 'There are a number of words which carry the sense of *wakefulness*, of being alert. *Vijnapitah* is one. *Jnana* is another. Then there's *Janati* or *Jagarah*, or even *Prajna*.'

"'They are well-known words among Sanskrit Scholars?'
"'And laymen, too.'
"'Don't use a Sanskrit word.'

"Again Adikaram halted. Krishnaji turned. 'To use it is to bring to the mind the ancient tradition and to sanction past comprehension. A Sanskrit word will attach what you are saying to the remembered texts. Tell it in your own way, in your own words, what you are seeing. Use modern Singhalese words.'[89]

The attempt to dress the inexpressible in words was a goal of Krishnamurti throughout his life. It was a central and characteristic feature of his own new path. In earlier years, he had already spoken about it, showing some anticipation of the future. After one talk, Sidney Field spoke with him about his own difficulty understanding Krishnamurti's point of view as well as about the problems he saw with Krishnamurti's use of words. Krishnamurti replied: "'Yes, I muffed it this morning, I'm trying to say something about a new dimension, to convey new meanings, but my words are interpreted in the old way. Like a painter expressing something new, I'm learning a new technique. It's not easy.' He paused for a moment and then added. 'But wait until I'm sixty....'"[90]

Throughout numerous conversations he tried to bring these new paths closer to people who were open. In these attempts, he addressed in particular the avant-garde of a 'New Science,' represented by personalities that included David Bohm, Rupert Sheldrake, Jonas Salk, Maurice Wilkins, and others. He had hoped that at least they would be able to understand his message; but after a brief period, he always reached a certain final point. For the most part, the discussions remained on an intellectual plane, due to the nature and background of his partners in the discussions, while he was talking from an enlightened consciousness. The gap was not to be bridged—one may ask for what reason. However, it is also conspicuous that no close relationships existed between Krishnamurti and those representing an esoteric tradition. The Dalai Lama seems to be one of the rare exceptions. Even in this case, however, Krishnamurti felt resentment, as I was told by Friedrich Grohe and based on a remark Krishnamurti had made on the evening of his second discussion with the Dalai Lama. Perhaps, through his attacks against the esoteric tradition, Krishnamurti had shut himself off from the group of people who would have been able to understand him better, from people with whom he had long, often fruitless discussions. One only has to study the long discussions Krishnamurti had with the psychiatrist Shainberg to realize that someone who could see was talking to a blind person. Krishnamurti's frustration is almost physically tangible. "We have tried for the last fifty years to see if a few could get out of the stream, get out without motive."[91] Perhaps, Krishnamurti realized this more than he thought—but more through his being than through his teachings. He once gave a wonderfully impressive example of it.[92] At an overcrowded Indian train station he happened to talk to a self-conscious man. After a few words, the man offered Krishnamurti a cigarette and Krishnamurti declined it. After a few minutes of silence, the man began speaking, questioning whether it really makes sense to smoke at all. Krishnamurti neither agreed with him nor told him to stop smoking. After that, fully determined, the man threw away his cigarettes and decided to stop smoking from that moment on. Krishnamurti told this little story as an example of spontaneous insight and for the realization of a deep understanding. Even then, he was too modest and so he did not even consider that it had been his influence on the man that had led to the change. Millions of smokers can see clearly that it is very bad for their health to smoke—but nevertheless they cannot stop smoking. Enveloped by Krishnamurti's spiritual force-field and touched at his innermost being, this man at the train station was able to take Krishnamurti's energy into himself in a way that made it possible for him to stop perhaps his worst vice. This insight did not come to him from his understanding of Krishnamurti's 'anti-smoking-campaign,' but because his encounter with the holy did make him as whole as was possible.

By 1929, Krishnamurti had dissolved the Order of the Star; in 1968 he founded the 'Krishnamurti Foundation.'

He must have realized that an organizational framework was necessary for his work. It is stated in the founding document that: "...the Krishnamurti Foundation is the new organization without the psychological belonging and dependence which most organizations bring about. This is very important to bear in mind in all the work we are doing together. Cooperation is necessary but the ugly and brutal side of organization has no part in what we are trying to do. There is a great deal to do which has never been done in the past. We must meet together at least once a year to talk things over as friends, express our problems and resolve them."[93] The Krishnamurti Foundation was founded after years of severe struggle with Krishnamurti Writings Inc. (KWINC), which had striven for its independence from Krishnamurti under the management of Rajagopal and which worked more often against Krishnamurti than according to his wishes. Krishnamurti often had the painful realization that general human weaknesses, like envy, jealousy, ambition, etc., could grow and spread around him too. Problems with the Krishnamurti schools came up, the individual branches of the Foundation fought against one another, teachers rose up against him—there was always a lot to do.[94]

If somebody from outside views the events of those times objectively, it seems evident that the weaknesses that appeared in these organizations founded by Krishnamurti mirrored those in the Order of the Star, perhaps with slight changes in emphasis. This insight explains why Krishnamurti released a memorandum from the Foundation that said: "Under no circumstances will the Foundation or any of the institutions under its auspices, or any of its members, set themselves up as authorities on Krishnamurti's teachings. This is in accordance with Krishnamurti's declaration that no one anywhere should set himself up as authority on him or his teachings."[95]

Considering all the misunderstandings he encountered, one may wonder why Krishnamurti did not withdraw completely and fulfill his old wish to become a sannyasin. He himself answered that question beautifully in England in 1980. "Then what is the motive? I think when one sees something true and beautiful, one wants to tell people about it, out of affection, out of compassion, out of love. And if there are those who are not interested, that is all right, but those who are interested can perhaps gather together. Can you ask the flower why it grows, why it has perfume? It is for the same reason the speaker talks."[96]

VII. The Revolutionary Sage

"...For there are in the world many untrue thoughts, many foolish superstitions, and no one who is enslaved by them can make progress. Therefore you must not hold a thought just because it has been believed for centuries, nor because it is written in some book which men think sacred; you must think of the matter for yourself, and judge for yourself whether it is reasonable. Remember that though a thousand men agree upon a subject, if they know nothing about that subject their opinion is of no value. He who would walk upon the Path must learn to think himself, for superstition is one of the greatest evils in the world, one of the fetters from which you must utterly free yourself."[97] If one did not know the source of these words, one could easily—and with reason—mistake it for a basic statement from Krishnamurti's post-messiah time. In my view, this early fundamental tone carries considerable significance.

Nearly twenty years later, in 1928, Krishnamurti shouted to his audience: "Do not become followers or disciples of individuals but become the tabernacle of Truth...."[98] Again we meet the contrast between individuality and universality. For many spiritual teachers, both aspects form a unity where the universality expresses itself through the individuality. However, for Krishnamurti, one can only trust in universality, the individual components are merely an obstacle to the revelation. During his early years, Krishnamurti once expressed this idea with brutal clarity: "One day, as I am really at the bottom very keen on it all, I shall take it up and do what *I* think is right and hang

61

everybody who has got any personal element in it."[99] When Krishnamurti did take a critical look at serious seekers, his criticism was sometimes more moderate, even showing an interest in esoteric philosophy. Once, during his talks with Rom Landau—in my view, the writer of the most informative publication about Krishnamurti—they talked about Rudolf Steiner. "I have never studied Steiner, and I wish you would tell me more about him. All I know about Steiner comes from Dr. Besant's occasional remarks. I think she had a great admiration for Steiner's unusual gifts, and was sorry that their relationship had to be broken, but I never studied him properly. As for occult perceptions, for me they are not particularly spiritual: they are merely a certain method of investigation. That's all. They might be spiritual at times, but they are not always or necessarily so.

"You have never read any of Steiner's books?

"No, nor have I ever read any of the other philosophers....

"But Steiner was not a philosopher.

"Yes, I know. I only meant writers of a philosophical or similar kind. I cannot read them. I am sorry, but I can't. Living and reacting to life is what I am interested in. All theory is abhorrent to me."[100]

Again we find ourselves confronted with one of the most peculiar aspects of Krishnamurti, his deep aversion to esoteric teachings; the esoteric tradition did not mean anything to him. The young Krishnamurti was reading Edgar Wallace while the members of the Order of the Star meditated on the 'Coming,' and the Krishnamurti of later years always visited the bookshelves with the detective stories at airports. Perhaps this inner separation and exclusion were necessary for Krishnamurti to find his own distinctive path. A movie was made about him in the eighties

called *The Seer Who Walks Alone*. This loneliness is of
course connected to his radicalism, a fact well known to
Krishnamurti. "Whether it's Buddha, Christ, the Pope, or
Mr. Reagan telling me what to do...I won't. This means
we have to be extraordinarily capable of standing alone."[101]
No other mystic, sage, or philosopher made such radical
requests—of himself and of others. This must have initiated a kind of elite character to his teachings because only
a few were willing to follow him, particularly because
many simply did not understand his words. But "those few
do count," as Krishnamurti said to Landau in confirma-
tion. He did not want to talk to people who "need a sani-
tarium," but as he said to Landau: "You must understand
that I can only talk to people who are willing to revolu-
tionize themselves in order to find the truth."[102] It touches
me in a rather strange way when I read the following sentence from the same talk: "I must confess that it makes
me sad that I cannot help as many people as I should like
to."[103] Was it a personal element which hindered the Christ-
impulse—to put a name to it—or did Krishnamurti's 'task'
require this kind of restriction? Krishnamurti's confession
should be considered in conjunction with the helpless plea
from one of his listeners: "I want only one thing, to know
the true purpose of life, and you shower me with things
that are beyond me. Can you not please tell me in simple
words what is the true significance of life?"[104] This shows
the tragedy of the revolutionary sage Krishnamurti—he
was not able to do so. He was, however, able to live the
answer. This shows us the deeper meaning of his attempt
when three years before his death, he tried using a light
metaphor to clarify this issue: "'You see,' K said, 'that's
the whole conception—that there are such people who
help. Not guide, not tell you what to do, because that's too

silly. But, just like the sun, give light. And if you want to sit in the sun, you sit in it. If you don't, you sit in the shadow.'

"'It's that kind of enlightenment,' Dr. Salk said.

"'It is enlightenment,' K replied."[105]

Many people came to Krishnamurti to ask him whether his path would be the right one. One of his answers was: "You have to know for yourself. If it seems honest to you, it certainly is so for you. But my own idea is different."[106] He preferred not to answer directly because he believed that nobody would be able to give the answer. "Can anyone else tell you what is true? Can anyone tell you what is God? No one can: you have to discover it for yourself."[107] This radicalism tempted Krishnamurti to make statements that were often marked by intolerance. His stated opinion about certain religious teachers, e.g., Maharishi Mahesh Yogi, which he often accused of clear materialistic greed, were sometimes simply awkward. Criticism is always acceptable but should be constructive, based on facts and not on an unreflected aversion. It sounds presumptuous when Krishnamurti, who often said about himself, "I am one with the beloved," or "I drank from the source," or "I realized unity," judges: "The moment the guru says he knows, then you may be sure he doesn't know."[108] This contradiction also appears in his attempts to disqualify 'book knowledge': "Do you seriously think you can learn from books?"[109] Why then, on the other hand, did he himself write books and published his talks? In this context I was struck by two messages of the Masters from the early years. One can be found in *At the Feet of the Master*: "Now that your eyes are opened, some of your old beliefs, your old ceremonies, may seem to you absurd, perhaps, indeed, they really are so. Yet though you can no longer take part in them, respect them for the sake of those good souls to whom they are still important. They have their place, they have their use; they are like those double lines which guided you as a child to write straight and evenly, until you learned to write far better and more freely without them. There was a time when you needed them; but now that time is past."[110] The second one is stated to be from the Master Kut Humi and was received by C. W. Leadbeater for Krishnamurti: "Of you, too, we have the highest hopes. Steady and widen yourself, and strive more and more to bring the mind and brain into subservience to the true Self within. Be tolerant of divergences of view and of method, for each has usually a fragment of truth concealed somewhere within it, even though oftentimes it is distorted almost beyond recognition. Seek for that tiniest gleam of light amid the Stygian darkness of each ignorant mind, for by recognizing and fostering it you may help a baby brother."[111] Both statements seem to me, with hindsight, like prophetic reminders of the possible danger. Perhaps Krishnamurti, in his radical attempt, did not pay enough attention to the limitations of mankind in its present state of evolution; perhaps he wanted too much too quickly. From a certain perspective the statement that "humility is unaware of the division of the superior and the inferior, of the Master and the pupil"[112] is correct but who except Krishnamurti was on a plane from which this sentence can be spoken righteously. Krishnamurti wanted to lead people to a freedom for which they were possibly not sufficiently mature. It was in this regard that Emily Lutyens wrote in desperation: "He had cut the ground from under mine (my feet, P.M.) and I felt I was dropping into nothingness."[113]

The 'reality' of which Krishnamurti spoke was not a reality Emily Lutyens and others were able to grasp. They were unable to follow Krishnamurti to the 'other shore.' She confessed: "But what was this reality? I no longer knew, and felt lost in what seemed to me cold abstractions, having no relation to the life we are called upon to lead here and now."[114] Emily Lutyens never found a connection to Krishnamurti's new paths again, but who would deny her the only criteria necessary according to Krishnamurti—sincerity? She nearly converted to the Roman-Catholic Church when she was older but in the end she was not determined enough to take this step. She was lovingly connected to Krishnamurti until she died, without understanding his path or his intentions. In a letter dated August, 1935, which remained unanswered, she expressed her criticism in a few moving sentences: "How do you know that you have not merely found an escape? You cannot face life as it is—figuratively speaking—you have always escaped ugliness by flying to the most beautiful places. You are always 'retreating.' You have found an escape that gives you ecstasy—but so have all religious mystics…. How can I, as an outsider, know that you are any more right than someone else who says they have attained ecstasy—God—Trust etc.? (There is no reply to this letter.)"[115]

Krishnamurti did not change the direction of his path. His demand for a radical freedom did not allow for the old paths with steps along the way. Even the shattering realization that nobody followed him into the 'pathless land' did not change his mind. He was to remain a lonely light in the darkness.

VIII. The Mystery

As indicated in its subtitle, this book is intended as an approach to the mystery of Krishnamurti. In this chapter I shed some light upon this mysterious, many-faceted being, who as a human personality was the bearer of the name Jiddu Krishnamurti. Those who have dealt with the esoteric, the mystic, the mysterious Krishnamurti will soon meet with a strange contradiction. The Krishnamurti of the post-1929 talks was factual, dispassionate, intellectual, and totally free of any 'phenomena.' The 'private' Krishnamurti was the exact opposite. He was inconceivable, filled with mysticism, enveloped by an aura of mystery, with an irresistible radiation—if he did not choose to withdraw due to his shyness—and characterized by an abundance of strange phenomena that were known in part by the term 'The Process.' We would probably know more about the mystery of Krishnamurti had he not posted the public Krishnamurti as a kind of shield in front of the private man and had the people around him, in a very peculiar way, not only presented the factual side of his being to the outside world. For these reasons it was decades before Mary Lutyens published the first complete documentation of his life and the publication of his *Notebook*—an internationally acclaimed mystic work—was almost stopped by a pure anti-esoteric panic. I think that over the next few years there will probably be many books or stories published that describe an abundance of esoteric situations that make it clear that Krishnamurti was much more than merely a simple, transformed being, as he described himself in his own teachings, but was also an initiate and a blessed mystic. This is the part of his being I attempt to unveil in this chapter.

Spiritual Healing

Krishnamurti had healing hands from his early childhood but he almost never used this gift in public. It was only in his early years that he indicated the strength of his healing power to others. In November 1917 he wrote to Annie Besant: "You might be interested to hear that I give treatments to Nitya's eyes. His sight improved a lot and he is even able to see with his right eye. Mister Fleming gave me lessons on healing and I am personally very interested in it.... At Mister Sanger's everybody is visiting me for their headaches and toothaches and, therefore, you might imagine how popular I am."[116] To those who understand Krishnamurti, these words clearly indicate how unpleasant this reputation as a miracle healer must have been to him. This kind of publicity was not part of his being. Another letter he sent to Emily Lutyens in September, 1932 illustrates this point further: "I tried to use my healing capabilities in two or three cases but I asked everybody not to talk about it. It went well. Hopefully, a blind lady will feel better soon."[117] In the following years Krishnamurti hid this gift even more. He intended to heal people in a holistic way, from the source of their spiritual being. He did not want to free them from their symptoms of illness only to see them return to their old lifestyles.

The best documentation of the healer Krishnamurti is the biographical book by Vimala Thakar on her encounter with him.[118] In this book, she comments on her illness and the healing process which Krishnamurti initiated and which also started her own personal transformation. According to Thakar, Krishnamurti did not seem to have a clear understanding of this healing process. "In fact I am not going to do a thing to you. It is the healing power, which is going to operate, if it operates at all. I do not know what that power is. I do not know how it works. So there is no reason to feel obliged to me. If healing takes place, it means healing has happened."[119] The description given by Vimala Thakar on the feelings she had during the treatment is similar of those classical experiences of patients of spiritual healers. "I saw that a very strong and forceful current of vibrations passed through the head and went through the whole body. The body became wonderfully relaxed. My eyes closed of their own accord. Krishnaji removed his hands. I tried to open my eyes. I could not focus them properly. It was like coming back from a land of peace and light."[120] In this context, the precise technical interpretation of the happenings may not be of importance. Why is it necessary to press the mystery of healing, the functioning of a power that I do not hesitate to call divine, into the boundaries of worldly matters or even of measurable entities? Krishnamurti himself commented on the happenings of healing in a way that seems far more appropriate to me. "Well—you know, I have had this healing power, or whatever it is, since my childhood. I rarely exercise it. But this time there was an urge to help. Of course Love played the major part in this healing. You know what I mean—Don't you?"[121]

The healing influence of Krishnamurti sometimes emerged in a very sublime way that did not involve laying hands on the patient or some similar act. For the people meeting him it seemed like an inner process of becoming whole. This process could start with the act of stopping smoking and could end with a deep spiritual experience while meditating, as Rom Landau reports in his book.[122] Pupul Jayakar experienced a healing touch by Krishnamurti that was similar to Landau's own experience. In my opinion, Krishnamurti made a particularly important remark that leads one to suspect that his extrasensory perception was much further developed than was generally assumed, especially by his European acquaintances. "He said: 'I can see if you want me to.' And so the words which for years had been destroying me were said. Saying them brought me immense pain, but his listening was as the listening of winds or the vast expanse of water. I had been with Krishnaji for two hours. As I left the room my body felt shattered, and yet a healing had flowed through me."[123] This healing touch initiated an inner transformation for Jayakar, similar to that experienced by Thakar and others. One may question whether Krishnamurti used his healing power only in those cases when he sensed or saw that the outer healing was combined with an inner healing, or whether he underestimated the transformational effect of his healing power. One possible key for understanding this is his shyness and modesty. He certainly did not feel an urge to be a spiritual healer in the classical sense. His intent was to heal the *spirit* but not necessarily to undertake spiritual *healing*.

Clairvoyance

As a child, Krishnamurti had a whole range of paranormal abilities. He was able to see people who had died, to see the aura, to read thoughts, and he knew the contents of letters without having read them.[124] All these phenomena did not interest him much. He seems to have regarded them much as another child might regard superior mathematical skills. However, the events of 1925 involving the perversion of spiritual powers seem to have induced a negative attitude in Krishnamurti towards clairvoyance, etc., as Mary Lutyens indicates: "He was so disgusted by Arundale's and Wedgwood's psychic revelation in 1925 that far from using these powers or developing them, he was determined from that time onwards to push them into the background if unable to suppress them altogether."[125] These reservations should not lead to the impression that Krishnamurti might have lost his abilities. On the contrary, there were many situations that cannot be understood without assuming that Krishnamurti was far more aware than an average person. For example, the women accompanying Krishnamurti to a small temple in Tetu experienced his dealings with powers or beings that they were unable to perceive at all. In the end he explained to them "he had 'done something' in the temple and spoken to it— whatever 'it' was—and it had stopped immediately."[126]

Upon entering a room for the first time, Krishnamurti would penetrate or clean it with his energy. If asked, he would also agree to do this for his friend's apartments, as reported by Friedrich Grohe in his recollections. Krishnamurti never lost these powers. Only a few days before his death, Scott Forbes experienced how Krishnamurti was able to penetrate a room with his energy and to change this room by doing so. He recalls: "He did something to the room. One could see him doing it, and the room was not the same afterwards. He had all the power and magnificence he had always had."[127]

Sometimes his spiritual capabilities appeared unexpectedly. For example, he amazed Sidney Fields in this way when he agreed to cancel a journey before Fields had mentioned any word about a change of plans.[128]

However, he did discuss the topic with great sincerity. Sidney Fields asked him once whether it wouldn't be more convenient for him to simply levitate. "I have the key to all that, but I'm not interested."[129] Regarding this topic, Krishnamurti was in harmony with classical Indian tradition, in which the guru urges the pupil to be careful not to become a slave of occult powers (siddhis) but rather to ignore them and to take the next step on the path to the divine source.

One last story about this topic is meant to illustrate these thoughts. "It was at the woods at Shanklen, where I was sitting with Krishna one day, that he said to me: 'do you see that little fairy?'—which of course I did not. He described to me a little fairy creature hopping around, and seemed surprised that I could not see it also. He was undoubtedly psychic, but he did not set any store by it or make any capital out of it. To him it was just another faculty, like singing in tune, of no importance."[130] It seems that Krishnamurti, dweller in two worlds, did not consider knowledge of what was hidden beyond the veil of the world as a source for inspiration and strength. Sharing his visions with others would not have led them to a deeper dependence on him—what he probably feared after his experiences with the Theosophical Society—but would have helped them to develop a deeper sense for the mysteries of the creation until they were able to lift the veil by themselves.

Even though Krishnamurti probably only used his higher senses and healing powers very rarely, there is no doubt about their existence. I know of no statement by Krishnamurti in which he denied these abilities nor any statement in which he refers to them as an illusion. Surprisingly enough, nobody, except a few Indians, has discussed this topic with him in depth. Another of these unbelievable phenomena connected to Krishnamurti.

The Masters

Before 1929 the Masters of the Hierarchy, as presented by the Theosophical Society, played an important role in Krishnamurti's life. The fact that he really did not mention them in his talks after the dissolution of the Order of the Star lead to the widely expressed conclusion that Krishnamurti had surrendered his phase with the Masters or simply that "the Masters were an illusion." This hasty resolution does not take into account the moving experiences that people had who attended his encounters with the Masters—and those encounters did not end with the year 1929. One should read the following sentences, without any preconceptions, to sense whether they illustrate truth or delusion. "The presence of the mighty Being was with me for some time and then They were gone. I was supremely happy for I had seen. Nothing could ever be the same. I have drunk at the clear pure waters at the source of the fountain of life and my soul was appeased. Never more could I be thirsty, never more could I be in utter darkness. I have seen the light."[131]—words from Krishnamurti. "With his entry the atmosphere was marvelously changed. We felt the presence of a supreme majestic Being and Krishna had a look of great bliss on his face."[132]—words from Nitya. These sentences do not speak of hallucinations but about deep contacts with the divine dimension.

Years later, in 1961, Vanda Scaravelli experienced an encounter with this dimension. "It was as if there were a powerful presence which belonged to another dimension."[133] After a meeting with Krishnamurti in 1978, Mary Lutyens happened to return to the meeting room. There "a power overwhelmed her" which was so strong that even years later she shivered when she thought about the incident.[134]

One cannot pretend that Krishnamurti did not talk about this other reality. On the contrary, he often made comments to his friends that made it clear that he knew about the beings surrounding him. "He looked at me for a long time and then he asked, 'are you trying to protect me?' He then raised his two arms in a significant gesture. 'There are far greater beings who protect me.'"[135] Even the elemental that protected his body when Krishnamurti had left it (which is discussed in the next section titled The Process) knew about this protection. "They have worked and worked for so long, so many centuries, to produce such a body."[136] Who were these 'they?'

Krishnamurti himself never gave a precise answer to this question. Hints appeared occasionally, often hidden in little stories he told to good friends. "He said that the night before he awoke from some great depth, with the word 'Lord of the World' resounding in him. There was tremendous light, stronger than the sun."[137] In this case—in the year 1959, thirty years after the dissolution of the Order of the Star—he again used terms from the vocabulary of the Theosophical Society.

Only in the time between his separation from the Theosophical Society and his search for his own new way did he harshly reject the Masters. From a theosophical point of view this behavior was explained by his Arhat initiation, at which time the Master withdraws all guidance from his pupil and the pupil must then make his decisions independently.[138] Krishnamurti resented this explanation because it only reaffirmed the old dependencies.[139] When Mary Zimbalist asked him one day why he did not speak about the Masters any more he answered: "There is no need now that the Lord is here."[140] He did not question his role as a World Teacher nor did he deny the existence of the Masters. To me, his reserve regarding everything having to do with the Masters reflects his concern that again something that was holy to him could become profane, a risk he did not want to take.

The Process

The experiences that are described as The Process can be regarded as the core of the mystery of Krishnamurti. European scholars, in particular, have nervously avoided any mention of these phenomena. It was not until Pupul Jayakar's biography was published that a sincere analysis of the events, based on eastern esoteric mysticism, was available. Pupul Jayakar's work highlights two important points. First, The Process is very important for the rising of the Kundalini and second, Krishnamurti spoke quite differently about the events involved in The Process to the members of the Indian Foundation than he did to the Europeans.

Many stories by Krishnamurti himself or by the people who looked after him are thoroughly documented elsewhere and so are not repeated in detail in this book. Instead I try to find some structure in The Process. How did it happen?

In general, Krishnamurti first sensed a certain sickness. He withdrew, lay down, and asked not to be left alone but that those present should not worry about the events they were about to witness either. Often he complained about headaches, then he announced he would be "going off." After that, he would leave his body which was then occupied by an elemental. The elemental often talked in a childish voice, did not recognize the people in the room, and asked naive questions. Towards the end of these events it said: "He is coming back. Do you not see them all with him—spotless, untouched, pure—now that they are here he will come. I am so tired but he is like a bird—always fresh."[141] Then the real Krishnamurti who had returned to his physical body spoke again. There was another being present that was only characterized as 'he,' without further explanations.[142] In addition, sometimes there was the vision of a face that was of great importance to Krishnamurti and which was referred to in his theosophical times as the face of the Maitreya.

This was the basic structure of The Process. In each particular occurrence some details might have been different, for example, the intensity of the pains varied, the duration or the atmosphere changed, or the time Krishnamurti needed to leave his physical body changed. Nearly always, however, those in attendance sensed the doings of a mighty spiritual power.

Some of these doings are described in letters by Krishnamurti. In February, 1924 he writes in a letter to Emily Lutyens: "Last ten days, it has been really strenuous, my spine and neck have been going very strong and day before yesterday, I had an extraordinary evening. Whatever it is, the force or whatever one calls the bally thing, came up my spine, up to the nape of my neck, then it separated into two, one going to the right and the other to the left of my head, til they met between the two eyes, just above my nose. There was a kind of flame and I saw the Lord and the Master. It was a tremendous night. Of course the whole thing was painful, in the extreme."[143] This is a classical description of the rising of Kundalini as explained many times in Indian literature. The unusual nature of the events resulted in the extreme pains which were connected to the rising of the Kundalini. At this point even Leadbeater could not solve the puzzle and he was not able to provide an explanation to Krishnamurti.[144] Perhaps something that happened in the forties and fifties (it started in 1937) may help to better understand the pains involved.

After years of intensive yoga, the Pundit Gopi Krishna, a Brahman from Kashmir, experienced the rising of Kundalini. For him too, this process involved terrible pain and the experience of inner fire. Several of his writings about this process sound very similar to those of Krishnamurti's experiences. After some time he realized that the Kundalini did not rise through the main channel, the *sushumna*, but through a parallel channel, the so-called sun nerve *pingala*. He was able to reduce the pain by opening the moon nerve *ida* and so extinguishing the inner fire.[145] I do not claim that this experience of Gopi Krishna provides a complete understanding of The Process but I think it is very interesting to compare the writings of Gopi Krishna with those of Krishnamurti. To me, the transformation of Krishnamurti seems to be the more dramatic one. Perhaps this is the reason for the differences between the pains and the duration of The Process.

Pupul Jayakar touches the rising of the Kundalini in her biography several times. Among other incidents she mentions the following: "This is possibly a reference to the opening in the scalp which in *Kundalini* Yoga is regarded as the *Sahasrara* or the *Brahmarandhra*—the fully opened thousand-petalled lotus, resting in supreme emptiness. With this opening comes union and final liberation for the yogin."[146] Jayakar and Nandini Mehta witnessed this process for the first time in the summer of 1948. Later, it seems, they must have had an intense discussion about Kundalini, chakras, etc., because a letter from Krishnamurti to Nandini stated the following: "The wheels (his use of the word 'wheels' refers to the *chakras*. P. Jayakar) of Ooty are working, unknown to any, and other things are taking place. It is so extraordinary, and words seem so futile. Days are too short and one lives in a day, a thousand years. Keep alive, aware, and don't let anything, whatsoever, smother the flame."[147] The comments in parentheses were added by Pupul Jayakar as she knew what Krishnamurti meant by the term 'wheels' and Krishnamurti referred to 'wheels' because he knew Nandini would understand this term. Therefore it seems that Krishnamurti knew more about The Process than most of his friends thought he did. This is clarified further in a short note by Ravi Ravindra who had asked Krishnamurti directly what was meant by the term The Process. Krishnamurti looked at him with a certain sadness and answered: "This is what everyone wants to know. Then they will start imitating it and faking it. No. It cannot be said."[148] He did not answer that he did not know but that he was not able (or did not want) to speak about it.

Leadbeater tried to explain the painful experiences of Krishnamurti during The Process as a change in the cells of his physical body. The incoming energy, which was intended to prepare his physical body so it could become a tool for the Maitreya, noticed 'resistance' by the cells and tried to transform them. Krishnamurti refused to discuss these phenomena in public for a long time. It was in the seventies that he found the initiative to speak about them. Then the theory of cell transformation came up again. During a discussion about The Process, Pupul Jayakar asked Krishnamurti: "Do you think that the physical brain cells, unable to contain or hold the immensity of the energy that was flowing into the brain, had to create the spaces in the brain to sustain it? Did there have to be a physical mutation in the brain cells themselves? Or was it like a laser beam operating on the brain cells to enable them to function fully and so contain the boundless?

"Krishnamurti replied, 'Possibly that was so....'

"I asked, 'Is it that we are witnessing the first mind that is operating fully, totally.' 'Possibly,' K said, 'and that is what has to be done with the children here (at the Rishi Valley School.)'"[149]

This discussion is consistent with the notes about The Process that Krishnamurti includes in his *Notebook* of 1961: "All this seemed to affect the brain; it was not as it was before."[150] The brain had to be changed to become a vessel for the new consciousness, an opinion which Krishnamurti emphasized in the following years, especially in his discussions with David Bohm.

His own life experience should have taught Krishnamurti that contrary to his own opinion there was a spiritual evolution, a continuously developing realization of reality. In the twenties he had talked about his unity with the Absolute, about his melting with the Beloved—he had always mentioned it as a kind of final experience. This explains why the Theosophists accused him of an Advaita philosophy. During the following years and until his death one witnessed several experiences of ever deeper penetration into a boundless consciousness, an ever deeper realization of an infinite reality. Only two years before he died he mentioned to Pupul Jayakar: "For the last year, there is a state, not measurable by words, not in the field of knowledge, immense, totally out of time."[151] The process had changed, had become less painful but it had not

79

stopped. The transformation continued. The finite can only approach the INFINITE on in-finite paths.

The Overshadowing

The difference between Krishnamurti in the fullness of his spiritual powers and Krishnamurti within the limits of his personality was difficult to fully comprehend. Marianne Ryzek collected a large number of impressions in her interesting book on Krishnamurti and was always confronted by this phenomenon.[152] After Krishnamurti took the speaker's platform, or became involved in a discussion, a strong power streamed through him, a power which in many cases was even apparent to those present. What kind of power was manifesting itself through Krishnamurti?

Since his early theosophical years, Krishnamurti was fully aware that his physical shell was not his real being. He was able to throw it off like a cocoon and to move upwards into spiritual realms. "Experimenting with myself, not very successfully at first, trying to discover how I could detach myself and see the body as it is. I had been experimenting with it for two or three days—it may have been a week—and I found that for a certain length of time I could quite easily be away from the body and look at it. I was standing beside my bed, and there was the body on the bed—almost extraordinary feeling. And from that day there has been a distinct sense of detachment, of division between the ruler and the ruled, so that the body, though it has its cravings, its desires to wander forth and to live and enjoy separately for itself, does not in any way interfere with the true Self."[153] This was in no way a kind of mediumistic trance but an action taken in full consciousness. Krishnamurti entered a super-consciousness rather than a sub-consciousness. In the thirties he wrote to friends in India, using a classical term: "I am taking a complete rest and going into samadhi."[154] When Krishnamurti entered the spiritual world the event must have been accompanied by special perceptions. It does not seem very likely to me that it was only the entering of an objectless, absolute Being. Unfortunately, Krishnamurti himself left very few hints about his out-of-body experiences, although one year before his death he remarked to Mary Zimbalist that 'someone' watched over his life. He never again spoke about 'something' or 'anything.'

In May 1977 Krishnamurti underwent minor surgery in Los Angeles. During this surgery he left his body to become witness to an unusual 'encounter.' He told Mary Zimbalist about it: "It was a short operation and not worth talking about, though there was considerable pain. While the pain continued I saw, or discovered, that the body was almost floating in the air. It may have been an illusion, some kind of hallucination, but a few minutes later there was the personification—not a person—but the personification of death. Watching this peculiar phenomenon between the body and death, there seemed to be a sort of dialogue between them. Death seemed to be talking to the body with great insistence and the body reluctantly was not yielding to what death wanted. Though there were people in the room this phenomenon went on, death inviting, the body refusing.

"It was not a fear of death making the body deny the demands of death but the body realized that it was not responsible for itself, there was another entity that was dominating it, much stronger, more vital than death itself. Death was more and more demanding, insisting and so the

81

other interfered. Then there was a conversation or a dialogue between not only the body, but this other and death. So there were three entities in conversation."[155]

What is particularly remarkable to me in this account is the use of the term 'entity.' Krishnamurti's experience was not a kind of abstract-mystical experience (like the light-visions in out-of-body experiences of re-animated people) but an observation of energy fields that were crystallized into forms or entities. Most likely, Krishnamurti would have been able to say more about these "meetings beyond the threshold" than he did and I agree with Mary Lutyens' point of view: "His sense of dissociation from his body was a phenomenon beyond one's understanding. He obviously knew more about himself than he had ever yet divulged to anyone, yet there appears to have been a great deal that he did not know. Even if he had known, could he have put it into words? He could feel 'The Other' but he did not seem to know what it was. 'The Other' was limitless, as he often said. If it could be expressed in words it would be limited...."[156] Mary Lutyens' indication that Krishnamurti himself was not fully knowledgeable is confirmed in his own words. In 1925, after the first 'overshadowing by the Maitreya,' he had already expressed his sincere wish to have been able to see the change in the expression of his face with his own eyes.[157] These transformations occurred more often over the years, sometimes with such an enormous amount of power that it was even frightening to the eye-witnesses. Vanda Scaravelli once made a note in her diary: "Just as we were sitting down, a different look came into his eyes for a few seconds. It was a look of strange immensity and such overwhelming strength that one felt out of breath." And on another day, "We were talking and suddenly that look spread out again. It was tremendous with the fire of destruction in it, and a flash of something incredibly strong, as if the essence of power and of all powers were focused in it."[158]

In her one-volume biography on Krishnamurti, Mary Lutyens gives another account of Vanda Scaravelli's diary: "There was a change in K.'s face. His eyes became larger and wider and deeper, and there was a tremendous look, beyond any possible space. It was as if there were a powerful presence which belonged to another dimension. There was an inexplicable feeling of emptiness and fullness at the same time."[159] This presence is different from Krishnamurti's out-of-the-body experiences. These were, in his own words, characterized as morphic energies, while the presence revealed itself more as an amorphic, impersonal power. Therefore, it does not amaze me that Krishnamurti gave this presence the names 'it,' the 'other,' or the 'Universe.' "'It is in the room,' said Krishnaji. 'I don't know whether you feel it—what is that?' and then a strange look entered his eyes. 'I must be awfully careful about this.'... 'Is it an external thing happening inwardly? The Universe pouring in—and the body cannot stand too much of it. As I am talking, it is very strong. Five minutes ago, it wasn't there.'"[160] Krishnamurti himself possibly did not know exactly who or what this 'it' was. Strangely enough, he never seems to have thought it could have been his own higher self (monad). He already used this expression for his astral body when he was outside his physical shell. A 'soul-spark mysticism' (Seelenfunken-Mystik) as found in the teachings of Meister Eckhart was apparently not a possible explanation for Krishnamurti. One could also imagine it as a union of The Spirit (nous) and The One (hen) in the tradition of Plotinos. Therefore, it is surprising that shortly before his death, Krishnamurti became fascinated by the old Maitreya-Theory once again. In India he had met many times with the well-respected pundit Jagannath Upadhyaya who had told him in one of their talks that he had found a prophecy about the coming of the Lord Maitreya in an old Tibetan manuscript (Kala Chakra Tantra) and in the manuscript even the name of Krishnamurti had been mentioned as the vehicle of the Lord. Apparently, Krishnamurti was deeply moved by this meeting even though he did not fully confirm what was said.[161] However, his spontaneous outcry after the pundit declared this overshadowing process as the manifestation of the Maitreya was quite remarkable: "The Maitreya cannot manifest, it would be like the sky manifesting. It is the teaching that manifests."[162] I believe at this point we are very close to the mystery of Krishnamurti—and interestingly enough we have returned to the beginning again. Annie Besant already knew about this secret manuscript which was possibly of central importance to Krishnamurti's whole life. Shortly before his death Krishnamurti came across this manuscript again. Who could believe this was just by chance; and what is the essential difference between the 'entity' Maitreya and his teaching?

Krishnamurti on Krishnamurti

The difficulty of documenting Krishnamurti's statements about himself and his life lies in the fact that he declared his own inability to remember anything about the first third of his life. One of the few pictures from the theosophical period of his life he remembered was a scene in Adyar after the Apostle Affair when he was asked by Annie Besant if he would accept Leadbeater, Jinarajadasa, Arundale, Wedgwood and herself as his pupils. Krishnamurti refused and replied that he

would only be willing to accept Annie Besant.[163] While Mary
Lutyens was preparing the material for the first volume of her
biography he was honestly trying to help her with personal
memories but with little success. Nevertheless, when photographs of people he had been close to were shown to him he
was generally able to identify and even name them. In such
cases a memory and a moment of recognition could appear
like a flashlight before his inner eye.[164] One of those incidents
happened at one of his visits to the headquarters of the Theosophical Society when he entered the familiar old rooms
again after being absent for almost half a century. "Then he
went to the room of Dr. Besant. Carefully he stood before her
chowki with its little desk, and walked around the room,
quiet, listening. Suddenly, he stopped before a large photograph of Leadbeater which hung on a wall. 'This was not
there in my time,' he said. Radha Burnier said it had been
placed there many years later. For minutes Krishnaji stood
before the portrait, gazing at it; then suddenly he raised his
hand and said, 'Pax, pax.' Then he turned to Radha Burnier
and walked out of the room."[165]

One of the many peculiar phenomena Krishnamurti is connected with is his memory problem. While public events left
almost no trace in his memory, inner processes always remained vivid and clear to him, even looking backwards in
time. So in 1969 he drew a connecting line between the
Krishnamurti of seventy-five and the boy Krishna. "'The
other night, while meditating, I could see that the boy still
existed exactly as he was, nothing had happened to him in
life. The boy is still as he was. The body still needs to be protected from evil.' He paused again, and said, 'I still feel protected.'"[166]

The question of an inner identity for Krishnamurti was apparently in no way connected to outer memories. In order to

understand himself, he did not have to look back through his lifetime and find his identity by studying data that could be verified historically. For Krishnamurti, a break never occurred inside his inner being. In a talk with Susunaga Weeraperuma, he once gave a convincing explanation for the missing memories. "Memory is stored in the brain cells. When the mind is fully transformed the very brain cells experience a mutation. It is a fundamental change which cannot be explained in scientific terms. Unless you have personally experienced this mutation you will not know what I am talking about."[167] Krishnamurti had changed; he had undergone a transformation. But who or what was it that initiated this total transformation that even included the structure of his cells?

Krishnamurti only spoke with great discretion about the power or the various entities who guided and protected his life. In general, he only spoke about 'it' or a 'something.' "There is something. Much too vast to put into words. There is a tremendous reservoir, as it were, which if the human mind can touch can reveal something which no intellectual mythology, invention, dogma, can ever reveal. I am not making a mystery of it—that would be a stupid childish trick, a most blackguardly thing to do because that would be exploiting people. Either one creates a mystery when there isn't one or there is a mystery which you have to approach with extraordinary delicacy and hesitancy. And the conscious mind can't do that. It is there. It is there but you cannot come to it, you cannot invite it. It's not progressive achievement. There is something but the brain can't understand it."[168] His reply to questions about this 'something' was always that the questioner would not be able to understand it. With sheer and shocking frankness he explained this limitation to Mary Zimbalist, the person who was closest to him in the last years of his life. "I won't die all of a sudden. I'm in good health, my heart, everything is all right. It is all decided by someone else. I can't talk about it. I'm not allowed to, do you understand? It is much more serious. There are things you don't know. Enormous, and I can't tell you. It is very hard to find a brain like this and it must keep on as long as the body can; until something says enough."[169]

Only in the last years of his life did Krishnamurti reveal how inseparably this 'something' was connected with his body. With this perspective, one should look at the following weighty statement he made nine days before his death: "You won't find another body like this, or that supreme intelligence, operating in a body for many hundred years. You won't see it again. When he goes, it goes. There is no consciousness left behind of that consciousness, of that state. They'll all pretend or try to imagine they can get into touch with that. Perhaps they will somewhat if they live the teachings. But nobody has done it. Nobody. And so that's that."[170] These sentences upset the members of all Foundations and the Indians and Americans would have preferred to keep them unpublished. The members of the British Foundation, however, took the point of view, as expressed in Mary Lutyens' biography as well, that it was Krishnamurti's particular intention to deliver these words to later generations.

In 1980, Krishnamurti had already spoken sentences of a similar radical nature in a message to Mary Zimbalist. Sentences, demonstrating a final state of consciousness, which he had not spoken of for several years. "With the arrival in Rishi Valley in the middle of November 1979 the momentum increased and one night in the strange stillness of that part of the world, with the silence undisturbed by the hoot of owls, he woke up to find something totally different and new. The movement had reached the source of all energy.

"This must in no way be confused with, or even thought of, as god or the highest principle, the Brahman, which are projections of the human mind out of fear and longing, the unyielding desire for total security. It is none of those things. Desire cannot possibly reach it, words cannot fathom it, nor can the string of thought wind itself around it. One may ask with what assurance do you state that it is the source of all energy? One can only reply with complete humility that it is so.

"All the time that K was in India until the end of January 1980 every night he would wake up with this sense of the absolute. It is not a state, a thing that is static, fixed, immovable. The whole universe is in it, measureless to man. When he returned to Ojai in February 1980, after the body had somewhat rested, there was the perception that there was nothing beyond this. This is the ultimate, the beginning and the ending and the absolute. There is only a sense of incredible vastness and immense beauty."[171] Going back half a century, these sentences are not so surprising when compared to the verbatim transcriptions of the Ommen Talks of 1929. There one can find the following remarkable sentence: "I maintain, without a shadow of doubt, that I am the whole, the unconditioned, not part of the Truth, but the whole."[172] Where is the difference between the Krishnamurti of 1929 and the Krishnamurti of 1980 or 1986?

In a discussion with Krishnamurti in 1979, Mary Lutyens and Mary Zimbalist tried to find out what the 'mystery' was all about. The following dialogues which took place before the quotations that contained those remarkable statements, will end this chapter, although they themselves are in many

88

ways a statement of helplessness. That is, statements of helplessness for both parties, that of the questioners and that of the one who attempted to answer. It is my special intention to confront this dialogue, which contains those words that have not been spoken since the days of the Buddha or of Christ, and expose the inner tension of the whole mystery. I selected some short but precise phrases from these longer dialogues.

"Right through life it has been guarded, protected. When I get into an airplane I know nothing will happen."

"Only when talking and writing does this come into play. I am amazed. The vacancy is still there. From that age till now—eighty or so—to keep a mind that is vacant. What does it? You can feel it in the room now. It is happening in this room now because we are touching something very, very serious and it comes pouring in. The mind of this man from childhood till now is constantly vacant. I don't want to make a mystery: why can't it happen to everyone?"

"If you and Maria (i.e. Mary Lutyens and Mary Zimbalist, P.M.) sat down and said, 'Let us inquire,' I'm pretty sure you could find out. Or do it alone. I see something; what I said is true—I can never find out. Water can never find out what water is. That is quite right. If you find out I'll corroborate it."

"It is like—what—what is the biblical term?—revelation. It happens all the time when I'm talking."

"Another aspect of this is that I feel that there is another kind of protection which is not mine. There is a separate form of protection, not only of the body. The boy was born with that peculiarity—he must have been protected to survive all he did. Somehow the body is protected to survive. Some element is watching over it. Something is protecting it. It would be speculating to say what. The Maitreya is too

89

concrete, is not simple enough. But I can't look behind the curtain. I can't do it. I tried with Pupul (Jayakar) and various Indian scholars who pressed me. I have said it isn't the Maitreya, the Bodhisattva. That protection is too concrete, too worked-out. But I've always felt protection."[173]

How was it possible that someone, who said about himself that he was "the Whole Truth" and later on would say that he had "touched the source of all energy," was fumbling to understand his own being in this way? Were there two different aspects of Krishnamurti speaking about two different realities? The answer cannot be found on the level of rationality. Intellectual reasoning will not be able to approach the mystery of Krishnamurti (or only up to a particularly low point). Only the like can recognize the like—therefore only an enlightened consciousness will be able to answer the yet-unanswered questions and to reveal the mystery of Jiddu Krishnamurti in the Light of Truth.

However—he who has found it will not talk about it; and he who talks about it has not found it. "It is a mystery; the moment mystery is understood, it is no longer mystery. One cannot understand the mysterious—it is too infinite. It is like looking around the corner. Do you see?"[174]

The Death

In summer 1985, although not having a very good constitution, Krishnamurti answered Mary Zimbalist's question regarding how much time 'it' would still give him with: "I think ten more years."[175] A statement by Pupul Jayakar contradicts these words. "It was in Rougemont, Switzerland, in July 1985 that the first intimations of his approaching death arose within Krishnaji. I had met him at Brockwood Park late in September. He had waited for me in the little kitchen off the West Wing of the old house. He said he had to tell me something very serious. 'Since Switzerland, I know when I am going to die. I know the day and the place, but I will not disclose it to anyone.' He went on to say, 'The manifestation has started to fade.'"[176] Should he again have spoken in a different way to the Indians than to the British and the Americans? What was the reason for these two contradicting statements that also differ from some other assertions he had made in Brockwood and that also provided evidence that he expected to live a few more years? It is not completely impossible that Pupul Jayakar might have misinterpreted some of Krishnamurti's statements, being more correct in hindsight than being accurate in interpreting Krishnamurti's own words. For me, it is more likely that Krishnamurti was surprised by his death. This would also explain his question of astonishment that he asked himself in a talk with Mary Zimbalist shortly before his death. "What have I done wrong?" Apparently, he thought that his mission was not yet over. It seems he did not remember one of his own prophecies made in New Delhi in 1967. "...and I will be until I'm ninety-two."[177] Only one more year and he would have fulfilled this prophecy.

Krishnamurti died in Ojai, California. On February 17, 1986, a few minutes past midnight, he left his physical shell. Some weeks earlier, he had already said good-bye to the earth, there, where everything started—on the beach of Adyar. "In the evening he went for his last walk on the Adyar beach where he had been 'discovered' long ago. At the end of his walk he bade a long good-bye to the four quarters, turning around full square—to the East, to the South, to the West, to the North—in that solemn farewell known as 'the elephant's turn' in ancient times."[178]

91

Part 2
THE TEACHING

IX. Religion

The religious mind is a state in which freedom and a vast,
everlasting love exists. Then, you can pass,
then the mind can enter a new dimension,
and there is truth.

The Religious Human Being

Krishnamurti was the most religious critic of religions who has ever lived. A world-wide ecumenical movement, which tries to integrate every denomination just to please everybody, was not possible for him. He rejected all forms of dogmatism, of religious authority—in the form of an office—and every variety of ritual or ceremony. For him, religion in its general form did not mean a path that brings people together but rather the central force for their fragmentation. "Please do not say that belief brings people together. It does not. That is obvious. No organized religion has ever done that. Look at yourselves in your own country. You are all believers, but are you all together? Are you all united? You yourselves know you are not. You are divided into so many petty little parties, castes; you know the innumerable divisions. The process is the same right through the world—whether in the east or in the west—Christians destroying Christians, murdering each other for petty little things, driving people into camps and so on, the whole horror of war. Therefore belief does not unite people."[179] For Krishnamurti, religion required a vast inner free space to be true. He regarded this space as endangered by any form of denominational religion. He even went so far as to place true religion—being re-ligio in its original form—nearer to science, because to him this seemed to be a guarantor for freedom. "Religion is a form of science. That is, to know and to go beyond all knowledge, to comprehend the nature and immensity of the universe, not through a telescope, but the immensity of the mind and the heart. And this immensity has nothing whatsoever to do with any organized religion."[180]

From his radical point of view it did not seem necessary to him to evaluate the reformist approaches of the different religions. Therefore, when he was criticized for not supporting Gandhi's initiative to permit the caste-less people, the Untouchables, to enter the temples, he responded by saying that he believed the whole dispute was senseless because "God is not to be found inside four stone walls."[181]

Krishnamurti's radical criticism of religion cannot be seen as the end of his own path. His statements in the twenties and thirties were already leading in this direction but in a somewhat milder form. "Religions are like distant wells. I don't say that they don't carry water; but I say that everybody has to dig his own well in his own garden. Only then do you have fresh water at home, and this is important."[182] He regarded himself and his criticism[183] as a direct follower of Christ and Buddha, if indeed he tried to justify his position at all within an historical context. He once mentioned to journalists from Reuters that neither Buddha nor Christ had requested divinity for themselves nor that they had intended to found a religion, all of these steps were carried out by their followers after their deaths.[184]

Krishnamurti never attempted to diminish Buddha or Christ but he rejected any form of cult worship because to him the biggest mistake one could make was to put the admiration of a person above their teachings.[185] In addition, he connected the danger of religious illusion and devotion to self-made deceptions with the enraptured form of worship.[186]

Of all religious figures of the past, Krishnamurti felt close only to one—to the Buddha. On the question who of all great religious figures in history had come closest to the truth from his point of view, he answered without hesitation "Buddha." However, he did not forget to add immediately that he, of course, would be no Buddhist.[187] In the late twenties he clad his admiration with effusive words: "He (Buddha) was a super-genius, the greatest of humans, and His disciples were also geniuses, they were the great men of their day."[188] He was not as close to Krishna or Christ and in the inner circle he even mentioned his doubts about the historical authenticity of the latter.[189] Christian mysticism did not mean anything to him, which is not surprising taking into account his refusal to read any spiritual literature. His only well-known Christian interlocutor was Ivan Illich, not to mention his brief meeting with the American mystic Flower A. Newhouse in the thirties. It is only through his lack of knowledge in this subject that one can come to accept a misunderstanding like the following: "But you see, the Christian mystics, as far as I understand it, are rooted in Jesus, in the Church, in the whole belief. They have never gone beyond it."[190] It seems Krishnamurti had never heard about the negative theology of Dionysios

97

Areopagita or about the God-Mysticism of Meister Eckhart.

His rejection of monasticism and the priesthood goes even further, though it is perhaps easier to understand this from his point of view. "Have you ever been in a monastery? No? I was in one for some time just to observe. And I watched and I listened. I sat there and did the things they did. It is really a cruel affair to take a vow of silence and never speak again—you understand all this? Never look at the sky, the beauty of trees, never communicate what you are feeling to another. In the name of service, in the name of God, human beings have tortured themselves to find heaven. That is a tremendously tortuous and torturing affair. And desire is at the root of all this. I wonder if you understand that."[191] Krishnamurti regarded self-castigation, asceticism, and other similar aspects of religious tradition as a kind of 'deal with God.' When he describes illumination as a 'non-predictable' happening, one is reminded of a Lutheran attempt. In fact, the real target of his criticism is the expectation and not as much the practices themselves. The expectation that one might find the ultimate truth by way of a certain prayer, mantra or ascetic discipline will actually hide it from the seeker. Therefore, Krishnamurti believed that the path of doubt (which in his view was indicated in Buddhism) was more likely to lead to the 'goal' than the path of faith (which he saw manifested in Christianity). In his view, the truly religious person was beyond all of these attempts. "The religious mind is something entirely different from the mind that believes in religion. You cannot be religious and yet be a Hindu, a Muslim, a Christian, a Buddhist. A religious mind does not seek at all, it cannot experiment with truth. Truth is not something dictated by your pleasure or pain, or by your conditioning as a Hindu or whatever religion you belong to. The religious mind is a state of mind in which there is no fear and therefore no belief whatsoever but only *what is—what actually is*."[192] For Krishnamurti, religion in its traditional form was characterized a great deal by 'determination' (Bedingtsein), by limitation and determining. The dogmatic frame of any denomination gives a certain 'truth,' but for Krishnamurti this was not the TRUTH. In his view, true religion was always new, a voyage of discovery which knows nothing of maps or a destination.[193] Above all, it was determined by true freedom. "Freedom comes when the mind experiences without tradition…. Religion comes when the mind has understood the working of itself. When the mind is quiet, very still— the stillness is not the peace of death; this stillness is very active, very alert, watchful. To find out what God— Truth is, one has to understand sorrow, and the struggle of human existence. To go beyond the mind there must be a cessation of the self, the 'me.' It is only then, that which we all worship, seek, comes into being."[194]

Because of his radical demands, Krishnamurti was often accused of being non-religious and even of being an atheist. I confront this accusation with two short statements by Krishnamurti which in my view characterize Krishnamurti's unique sensitive spirituality. After he had presented his usual criticism in a discussion, he added the following: "If you really believed in God, if it were a real experience to you, then your face would have a smile; you would not be destroying human beings."[195] Krishnamurti made the second remark during a conversation with teachers in Varanasi where he talked about the future of his schools. "There must be truthfulness, fearlessness. The child must put his hands to the earth, there must be in him a quality of otherness."[196] Here we touch Krishnamurti's soul, his innermost being that was filled with the holiness of the unending SPIRIT and which sensed the hidden presence in all life.

Only rarely did Krishnamurti present the world with these insights into his deepest feelings. To prevent that which was holy to him from desecration—as had happened to him in his early years—he concealed it from the immature eyes of the world. Unfortunately, he concealed it so perfectly that one was led to suspect that it did not exist at all. For example, he was frequently criticized for his comments about 'not being influenced,' about his freedom from any written records regarding the question of religion and tradition. One of his most profound critics in this direction, but one who respected him otherwise, was the great Buddhist sage Lama Anagarika Govinda. In a conversation with Renée Weber he once summarized his criticism in the following way: "We are all influenced by many people; we all have to be grateful to many people. Why not admit it? Instead of talking about being unconditioned, one should say, 'I have to be universally conditioned,' that is, conditioned not by one thing or a few things but by all things. We are all conditioned. It is better to admit it. The mistake, or failure, of most people is that they think only of one or two elements that condition us, not of the infinite conditioning to which life subjects us. But if we could see the whole of our conditioning, then we really would be greater than any of those things. No person in the world can be unconditioned. It's impossible. Nor should he wish to be. For such an idea contradicts the whole life—renders it meaningless and invalid. Rather, we should always aim that our conditioning be by the whole, which is infinite."[197] With the last sentence, these two great religious personalities came together again, for Krishnamurti would have accepted that one—but only that one. He had seen the *Whole*, was filled by the *Beloved*, how could he talk of anything less? In my view, Krishnamurti himself hands us the key to his religious being in his deep talks with Rom Landau. During the fifty years that followed those conversations he never strayed from the path he had outlined then and so in some sense they can be regarded as the 'confession' of his religious life. "You are right. They live in the plains and I live, as you call it, on the mountain top; but I hope that ever more and more human beings will be able to endure the clear air of the mountain top. A man infinitely greater than any of us had to go his own way that led to Golgatha; no matter whether his disciples could follow him or not; no matter whether his message could be accepted immediately or had to wait for centuries. How can you expect me to be concerned with what should be done or how it should be done? If you have once lived on a mountain top, you cannot return to the plains. You can only try to make other people feel the purity of the air and enjoy the infinite prospect, and become one with the beauty of life there."[198]

Esoteric

Though he came from an esoteric tradition himself, to which he probably owed more than he was ever conscious, Krishnamurti strongly rejected the esoteric path and its view of the world, a rejection that brought him resolute and often well-justified criticism.

As I read them, I often wonder about some of the harsh attacks he made on the wide field of the esoteric. For example, once he answered a rather stupid question from one of his listeners with the remark: "Do not bother about angels. This is another way of escaping the conflict of life. To discuss angels is an unhealthy attitude from my point of view."[199] No hint about the possible reality of another realm of evolution, no mention of the moving experiences involving angels throughout history and even today, no thought about a possible brotherhood between angels and mankind.

He made similarly disapproving statements about the existence of the Masters and, after 1929, he often said that it was totally unimportant whether they existed or not.[200] Occasionally, as I read through Krishnamurti's answers on these topics, I ask myself whether he really did not want to see how unrealistic they sometimes were. For example, in Madras in 1947 he said: "...it would be a really beautiful world, if there were no teachers and no disciples."[201] Even with the educational background of this statement in mind, there remains a certain naïveté about the possibilities for human evolution. It simply was, and still is, an illusion to believe that all human beings, no matter what their level of inner maturity, can find illumination here and now. This was also a point made by Geoffrey Hodson, one of his most benevolent and most educated critics: "He (Krishnamurti, P.M.) seems either to be unaware of or deliberately to ignore the fact that without detailed guidance the majority of men are totally incapable of self-illumination."[202] Also, sentences like "all books in this world, including the holy books, are filled with theories,"[203] are not very helpful. What is the point of denying the whole spiritual inheritance of humanity? Freedom of spiritual quest also includes the freedom of choice and the freedom to keep the real.

Looking at the 'spiritual circus' of the late twentieth century, with its greed for something new, with its over-stimulation and its commercialization of religion, one might totally agree with the following sentence by Krishnamurti: "Can greed, whether for God, money or drink, ever become non-greed?"[204] But here, too, one has to keep in mind that even parasitic growth can only grow on a stem that is filled in its innermost by the divine. Perhaps the great mission of Krishnamurti would have been even greater had he reformed the esoteric rather than condemning it. However, the sword of differentiation does not work as a plow or for cutting trees.

God

Krishnamurti was often accused, or at least suspected by the orthodox, of being an atheist. However, his provocative wording did make it easy for his opponents (intentionally?) to level such criticism at him. He called 'God' a human invention, an anthropomorphous image and a product of exploitative priests. If one reads his books superficially, one might really be led the impression this was his view of God; but he clearly differentiated between 'God' and GOD. He preferred expressions like 'my beloved,' the 'nameless,' the 'life,' or the 'source.' "I have never said there is no God. I have said that there is only God as manifested in you... but I am not going to use the word God... I prefer to call this Life."[205] He did not fail to point out to his listeners the inadequacy of any wording. "It is no good asking me who is the Beloved. Of what use is explanation? For you will not understand the Beloved until you are able to see Him in every animal, every blade of grass, in every person that is suffering, in every individual."[206] Some years later during a talk at the University of Oslo, he clarified his position on God: "To me there is God, a living, eternal reality. But this reality cannot be described; each one must realize it for himself. Anyone who tries to imagine what God is, what truth is, is but seeking an escape, a shelter from the daily routine of conflict."[207] About fifty years later and based on his revolutionary teachings, he again answers a question on the discernibility of God: "I think it is possible, if one can free the mind of all belief—of all traditional acceptance of the word 'God' and the implications and the consequences of that word. Can the brain and mind be totally free to investigate that which the Israelis call the 'nameless,' the Hindus 'the Brahman,' the 'Highest Principle?' The whole world believes in the word 'God.' Could we put away all beliefs? Only then is it possible to investigate."[208] Only one year earlier, during his first talk in Saanen in 1980, had he formulated one of his most radical statements about God: "If man is the creation of God, God must be a rather horrible entity, a monstrous entity that is making human beings go through hell—right? He must be total disorder because we live in disorder, if he created us."[209] But trite sentences like this one did not help much to clarify Krishnamurti's true conception of God. He wanted to keep the absolute free of any kind of anthropomorphization; he wanted to distinguish the very source from the chaos that he believed was the result of human freedom. Therefore, I contrast these words spoken in Saanen with some of his more meditative thoughts from the same year and spoken in Bombay. "It is not that the beginning was chaos. That is impossible. Even if there is God—I am using God in the ordinary sense of the word— and he created the original chaos and out of that created order, the origin must have been order. It could not be disorder and out of that to create order. And man called it chaos and out of that man brought about tremendous disorder."

"Now he seeks to go back to that origin, that order. The state must be something of immense benediction, an immense, timeless, incorruptible state, otherwise it is not order."[210]

Krishnamurti wanted the holiness of God to be taken seriously. Therefore, one has to examine with great care whether his statements are about 'God' or GOD. Only then can one be sure to have understood Krishnamurti correctly—and it is then that one senses the reverence for the boundless Holy in his words. It is moving to read the conversation between Krishnamurti and some children as he tries to explain the nature of the Divine. With wonderfully poetic words he guides them through the mysteries of creation, in which the nature of the Divine appears, and he closes with the words: "Then behind it all there is something much deeper. But to understand that which is deep and beyond the mind, the mind has to be free, quiet. The mind cannot be quiet without understanding the world around you. So you have to begin near, begin with little things, instead of trying to find out what God is."[211]

The holiness of God and his reverence for Creation had a much stronger influence on the thinking and being of Krishnamurti than most of the people whom he influenced intellectually ever realized. In his innermost being, Krishnamurti was a Bhakti, aroused in his love for God and Creation. For these reasons I believe it was perfectly in character that his final words during his last public talk were about this mystery. "The origin is nameless; the origin is absolutely quiet.... Creation is something that is most holy, that's the most sacred thing in life...."[212]

Individuality

The self is no permanent entity, but a river, a running water.

It is not easy to explain Krishnamurti's views about individuality, the self, ego, the I and Atman, in a clear way. The Adyar-Theosophy of the Leadbeater-Besant era had a point of view that is so poetically expressed in *Light on the Path*: "You will enter the light, but you will never touch the flame."[212a] But in 1927 Krishnamurti said: "It lies in the power of each one to enter into the flame, to become the flame."[213] His sympathies for the Buddha become clear in his thoughts about the self. Similar to the beliefs of many Buddhist groups, Krishnamurti showed a tendency towards the Anatman doctrine that does not accept an immortal individuality (recently however, both the Dalai Lama and Lama Anagarika Govinda have stated a different opinion.) As he often emphasized, for Krishnamurti there was no self, no supra-self in the sense of the Atman-doctrine, and certainly no soul in the Christian sense.[214] In his autobiography, Alan Watts writes about an interesting conversation he had with Krishnamurti in Ojai (1953) during which Krishnamurti tried to explain to him in detail why there would be no 'he' who could find illumination. Krishnamurti then continued to explain what would happen when 'he' had made this experience. This wording led Watts to ask the thoughtful question whether this was a contradiction or whether it was simply a linguistic restriction that led Krishnamurti to use these words.[215]

For me, Krishnamurti's deepest quotes on the topic of the self/non-self can be found in an article by E. A.

Wodehouse that was published in 1930 in the International Star Bulletin. This article contains sentences that Krishnamurti uttered in total independence from the theosophical influence and while at the peak of his own spiritual insight. Among others one reads:

"It is wrong to regard liberation as annihilation. It is more truly a beginning... But this 'self' (in its liberated form, P.M.) is not an Ego. It is that far more subtle thing—individual uniqueness.... It is individual and at the same time it is universal.... For a human being there can be no complete merging in the Absolute, in the sense of evaporation into the Totality of Life. The differentiation, however abstract and tenuous, involved in this individual uniqueness is everlasting.... For, when once it (the Life, P.M.) has been purified of all egoism, it becomes, one may say, a new window through which the universal life can realize itself."[216] I believe that Krishnamurti attempted to distinguish the cognition of REALITY so radically from all human limitation that his wording sometimes took on a very negating touch that could lead (and did lead some of his 'followers') to the assumption that Krishnamurti represented a philosophy that encouraged the dissolution of any kind of individual consciousness. The delicate but crucial nuance in Krishnamurti's view becomes clear in his remarkable conversation with Alain Naude and Mary Zimbalist shortly after the death of John Field. In that conversation Krishnamurti explained that he questioned the assumption that the separate being, John Field, had ever existed. Rather, he had been an accumulation or an amassing of different aspects—thoughts, feelings, etc. The Buddhist Skandha teaching appears here. The true nature of John Field, then of course no longer 'John Field,' reveals itself only when he frees himself from the 'stream,' Krishnamurti's synonym for the wheel of reincarnation.

There is a suggestion of 'individual uniqueness,' but I have to admit that it is not possible to reach a final conclusion about the question of individuality based on Krishnamurti's statements.[217]

Immortality

Eternity is a constant beginning.

When Krishnamurti's brother Nitya died in 1925, Krishnamurti had felt his presence as an undeniable nearness of his beloved brother who now lived in a different dimension. Yet only a few years later he criticized his listeners and rejected all questions about a life after death as unimportant. This reaction left Emily Lutyens with deep uncertainty.[218] When questioned directly about a life after death, he answered: "No one knows the answer."[219] Only rarely did Krishnamurti speak about this issue in a definite way. He did not agree with the theosophical point of view on the continuance of existence in an astral body, though he explained to his friend Sidney Field after the death of John Field that the latter was "standing right next to him."[220] He called the part of the personality that survived the physical death a form of 'echo' that could reverberate for a long time but would cease in the end. Again, we are confronted with the problem of language. To Krishnamurti, immortality did not mean the eternal continuity of existence of a limited personality but a transformation into a totally different reality. In 1935 he answered a question about immortality as follows: "Now I can say there is immortality, to me it is a personal experience.... Immortality is the infinite present."[221] Krishnamurti answered questions that were asked from daily consciousness from a different (enlightened) level of consciousness. This is confusing but does not necessarily lead one astray. However, to understand his answers one must engage a method of intuitive sensing rather than of intellectual reflection.

Reincarnation

Now is the moment of eternity.
If you understand this, you have transcended all laws,
all limitations as well as karma and reincarnation.

Having read the last two sections one may be able to guess Krishnamurti's thoughts about reincarnation. "If nothing permanently exists, then nothing reincarnates."[222] Because the personality, from Krishnamurti's point of view, was only a 'series of reactions'[223] and not a continuing being, it was not possible for it to evolve. In the chapter on 'Evolution,' I consider this problematic perspective in detail.

Prayer

Krishnamurti's religious life, his entire life, lacks the aspect of the dialog. This is exemplified by the way he gives talks, which are more the monologues of an enlightened consciousness; and this holds true also for most of his conversations (even though there are moving exceptions) during which his attempt was to lift his partner onto his level. Krishnamurti never met them on their level.

This missing door to the 'You' also explains his attitude to prayer, which he regarded as useless. "Great strength does not come through prayer, it does not come through illusion, faith; it comes through clarity, through the mind that can see clearly."[224] Again, we find a total misunderstanding of the religious path, which cannot even be assigned to a particular group, for prayer, in different forms, is known in all world religions—including Buddhism. Perhaps it is prayer that expresses most clearly the aspect of devotion, of knowledge about being a creation. Krishnamurti's view was quite different: "Meditation is not prayer. Prayer implies supplication, begging, and that is utterly immature. You pray only when you are in difficulties. A happy man doesn't pray. It is only the sorrowful man who prays, the man who is asking for something, or who is afraid of losing something."[225] A statement like this one totally misses the religious life of countless people. I cannot understand how a man as sensible as Krishnamurti was unable to sense the deep inner touch by a divine reality from which a spontaneous prayer can emerge. It is the human, filled by true bliss, who finds in prayer his only way of expressing thanks to that REALITY in which he realizes the very source for his bliss.

X. Society

Throughout his countless journeys, Krishnamurti observed the surrounding world with great awareness. He talked to people from large cross-sections of the population, from the Dalai Lama to nuclear weapons technicians in Los Alamos. Everywhere he found inner conflict, open or hidden violence, fear and insecurity. To this world, which seemed to drown in hopelessness, he countered with a message of holiness and wholeness of life, to be accomplished by reverence and love for any living being. All life is one—we are this life—this life is holy We always find these postulates when we analyze Krishnamurti's statements about certain social problems.

Education

Krishnamurti regarded the art of education as very special. The teacher, in a sense, has the future of humanity in his hands. It is up to him to develop the "individual uniqueness" of each child, of which Krishnamurti had already spoken very early in his life. To live up to this task, the teacher must know about his own qualities and is then able to fulfill his task with inner security. "Only when the educator himself feels the dignity and the respect implicit in his work, will he be aware that teaching is the highest calling, greater than that of the politician, greater than the princes of the world."[226] Krishnamurti regards such self-respect by the teacher so

111

highly because it grants the teacher an inner independence.

Education should always be creative, always new, taking into account the individual child. Krishnamurti disapproved of any form of copying of a certain method or a formative influence of any kind of ideology. "When one follows a method, even if it has been worked out by a thoughtful and intelligent person, the method becomes important, and the children are important only as they fit into it."[227] This advice is also a reminder for parents who can make crucial mistakes in the educational sphere if they make particular demands on their children. Similar to following certain educational methods, setting goals can imply the erection of insurmountable barriers to a true education. Comparing the children in a family, reducing them to the same level and often with the most successful child as the model, is a dramatic mistake in Krishnamurti's view. "This comparison is a form of violence.... Imitation is violence."[228] Because the family is only a reflection of society on a small scale it cannot be changed without realizing and correcting this elementary mistake. Education must be transformed totally, it must be revolutionized.

By the latter half of the fifties Krishnamurti had expressed this idea in a programmatic way: "Education today helps only to cultivate memory. We are turning human beings into memory machines. We are turning out mediocres who can retain facts and opinions and draw on them when need arises. We are turning out men whose minds are conditioned by traditions, beliefs, religions, etc.

"It seems to me that real education begins when you get beyond all such conditioning factors; when you understand the process of thinking.

"Society is not going to help you in your efforts to get beyond conditioning factors. Society wants to breed mediocres in order to maintain its traditions. You will have to revolt against such society."[229]

Long before the times of 'holistic thinking,' Krishnamurti demanded the holistic approach in his form of education. Only if the individual child is educated according to the dignity of his or her unique wholeness can the process encompass his or her true inner being, only then can the inner wholeness communicate with the outer in complete harmony. In a letter, dated March 15, 1979, Krishnamurti states this idea in his inimitable precision. "This sensitivity to the fallen leaf and to the tall tree on a hill is far more important than all the passing of examinations and having a bright career."[230] The child becoming an integral whole, developing in a holistic way, would be accompanied by becoming whole and by a healing process of the relationship between humanity and nature, a process that cannot be accomplished by outer acts. According to Krishnamurti, a change of society can only evolve from the inner to the outer and for him education was the key to this change.

Politics

"So you are the world and the world is you, very profoundly."[231] This sentence, so often quoted yet so rarely understood, contains Krishnamurti's entire political program. One who understands in the depth of his consciousness that he does not exist separately from the world must take inner leave of any form of separatism or nationalism. In Krishnamurti's view, any form of 'ism' prepares the ground for the separation of people, independent of any worldly or a super-worldly authorization. "If you see, as the speaker saw many, many years ago as a boy, that nationalism is a poison and immediately ceased to be a Hindu—you will be finished with all those superstitions and all the rubbish that goes on in the name of nationality."[232] A little bit later, he stated this danger even more dramatically: "This identification with various countries, various cultures, is an isolating process and causes division and therefore war."[233] With such a world-view, fascism or dictatorships are not 'divine punishments' or 'undeserved punishments,' but are examples of the consequence of the accumulated inner violence of many people. This context should be kept in mind when reading statements by Krishnamurti like "politics is deadly."[234] In Krishnamurti's view, politics was a deeply corrupt social authority and so was an unsuitable sphere of activity for religious people: "A truly religious man is not concerned with politics; to him there is only action, a total religious action, and not fragmentary activities which are called political and social."[235]

Again, one must take into account Krishnamurti's educational ideal to interpret his criticism of the political system correctly. For him, change could only emerge from the individual, from the inner being of the individual, and not from any social institution. "Systems, whether educational or political, are not changed mysteriously; they are transformed when there is a fundamental change in ourselves. The individual is of primary importance, not the system; and as long as the individual does not understand his total process, no system, whether of the left or of the right, can bring order and peace to the world."[236] Inner chaos leads to outer chaos and outer chaos leads to war.

War

"The individual identifying himself with a community, with a nation, with a race, with a religion invariably brings conflict between human beings. It is a natural law. But we are only concerned with the effects, not with the causes of war, causes of this division."[237] The reasons for this came from the people themselves. "The war within you is the war you should be concerned about, not the war outside,"[238] was a message he repeated many times in Ojai during the war year 1941. This was language that was almost impossible to convey in a patriotic California and in times of war hysteria. The same holds true for his statement that, in his view, there was no difference between the then-recent aggressions of Germany and England's many decades of imperialism. He believed that all states involved in the war were equally responsible because none of them was peaceful internally. As a German author, I am especially doubtful whether Krishnamurti, in his Californian isolation, truly realized or even suspected the real horror and the incomprehensible inhumanity of the Nazi-regime.[239] Krishnamurti did not answer directly the specific question about his reaction to an aggression by the state, as for example, in Hitler-Germany. But he answered indirectly, with almost the same wording as in the Sermon of the Mount: "I don't think any evil can be overcome by brutality, torture or enslavement; evil can be overcome by something that's not the outcome of evil. War is the result of our so-called peace which is a series of everyday brutalities, exploitation, narrowness and so on. Without changing our daily life we can't have peace, and war is a spectacular expression of our daily conduct. I do not think I have escaped from all the horror, but only there's no answer, no final answer, in violence, whoever wields it. I have found the answer to all this, not in the world but away from it. In being detached, the true detachment which comes from being, or attempting to be, more (word left out) to love and understand...."[240]

I do not want to take it upon myself to judge whether Krishnamurti's point of view is unrealistic or not. He may claim to have great eyewitnesses from the past, but in the end everybody has to answer this question in his own heart. For the quest, one meditative stimulus may be added which also leads into the depths of Krishnamurti's being and which is one most worthy to think about in this field. "We love to kill each other. This killing of other human beings has never stopped throughout the history of man's life on this earth. If we could, and we must, establish a deep long abiding relationship with nature, with the actual trees, the bushes, the flowers, the grass and the fast moving clouds, than we would never slaughter another human being for any reason whatsoever. Organized murder is war, and though we demonstrate against a particular war, the nuclear, or any other kind of war, we have never demonstrated against war. We have never said that to kill another human being is the greatest sin on earth."[241]

Science and Technology

Krishnamurti is counted amongst the most radical critics of a society that believes in science, of a society that overlooks the growing moloch of inhumanity that lies behind it's blinded view through the splendor of new inventions. Modern technology, with all its virtually inestimable consequences, has developed a momentum which Krishnamurti considered to be very dangerous.

"The world is becoming something totally new. Space is being conquered, machines are taking over, tyranny is spreading....

"Something new is going on of which we are not aware.... You are not aware of the movement, the significance, the flow, the dynamic quality of this change. We think we have time.... There is no time...the house is burning."[242]

Krishnamurti was no apostle of the Stone-Age. He definitely saw the positive aspects of technological evolution. It would be silly, he once said in an interview with Susunanga Weeraperuma, "to use bullock carts in the age of jets."[243] The solution was not to be found in a fearful step backwards but in the conscious realization of the possibilities and limitations of a modern industrial society in general and scientific thinking in particular. Scientific thinking has to change its parameters, it has to be open for a transcendence yet to be discovered, and it must enter into the—much discussed—paradigm change. Science must form a 'holy union' with the religious consciousness. "When the scientific mind breaks through the limitations of the known—then perhaps it approaches the religious mind."

"The scientific mind with its logic, its precision, its inquiry, investigates the outer world of nature, but this does not lead to an inward comprehension of things; but an inward comprehension brings about an understanding of the outer. We are the result of the influences of the outer. The scientific mind is precise and clear in its investigations. It is not a compassionate mind, for it has not understood itself."[244] Krishnamurti stated his opinion even more specifically in a dialog with children of the Rishi-Valley-School: "A new mind is only possible when the religious spirit and the scien-

tific attitude form part of the same movement of consciousness."[245]

A technological world view (dominated by technocrats)
which reduces men to machines and spiritual problems to
the question how to fix things misses the true essence of
humanness. The inner life, the real life for Krishnamurti, is
not only unrecognized by this world view but, even worse,
is hindered in its development. Science and technology
strive for a position which only religion in its pure, non denominational, sense is entitled to. "Technical knowledge,
however necessary, will in no way resolve our inner, psychological pressures and conflicts; and it is because we
have acquired technical knowledge without understanding
the total process of life that technology has become a
means of destroying ourselves. The man who knows how
to split the atom but has no love in his heart becomes a
monster."[246] Those words, written only ten years after
Hiroshima, echo throughout the world as a reminder even
today; even though the dangers of nuclear technology appear less frightening today than in times past. Nuclear fission can only be seen as a metaphor for an inner fission, an
inner disunity of the human being. Only if this fission can
be overcome, if wisdom and science can find a unity in the
individual,[247] only then will a more humane and loving society emerge.

Animal Protection

It is very unusual to find statements by Krishnamurti that
are spoken as a strict rule. It was more his way of philosophy or his form of education to lead people to their own
path by using multiple negations. By showing what *some-*

thing was not, he still left his listener free to decide for himself what *it* was instead.

However, Krishnamurti did not follow this way of action in any discussion about the rights of animals in society. In this case he stated his opinion very directly. The ethics of the Old Testament with its attitude of "fill the earth and subdue it" was a perversion of the meaning of creation to him. He regarded butchering, hunting and vivisection as a perversion of human nature and as the brutal signal for a humanity that has gone astray. Sometimes, he was quite brusque in personal encounters on this topic. "Sir, I know from your breath that you eat meat. Don't eat it. It is poison!"[248] Unfortunately, Weeraperuma does not write about the reaction of Krishnamurti's partner in this conversation, which might have given us more insight into this vehement statement.

In one of his Letters to the Schools, dated February 1, 1980, Krishnamurti writes about cruelty: "In western countries you see birds carefully nurtured and later in the season shot for sport and then eaten. The cruelty of hunting, killing small animals, has become part of our civilization, like war, like torture, and the acts of terrorists and kidnappers. In our intimate personal relationships there is also a great deal of cruelty, anger, hurting each other. The world has become a dangerous place in which to live and in our schools any form of coercion, threat, anger must be totally and completely avoided for all these harden the heart and mind, and affection cannot coexist with cruelty."[249] Again, it becomes clear that Krishnamurti viewed life as a unity and that the treatment of one species by another was the reflection of a detail that exists in the whole. Cruelty cannot be parceled out, it is either apparent in the whole, indivisible, or it is totally overcome. Human endeavor should only be concerned with *total* over-coming.

The depth of Krishnamurti's concern with this rift in the attitude of men regarding nature and the animal kingdom becomes even more clear with the words he wrote on the topic at the very beginning of his *Last Journal*. Those sentences, written in an almost meditative consciousness, do not attack but rather touch the innermost being of every human. Those few sentences, reminiscent in character of the Sermon of the Mount, not only call upon the individual to act but they also include a social manifesto. Words that should be heard and understood in silence. "It is odd that we have so little relationship with nature, with the insects and the leaping frog and the owl that hoots among the hills calling for his mate. We never seem to have a feeling for all living things on earth. If we could establish a deep abiding relationship with nature we would never kill an animal for our appetite, we would never harm, vivisect, a monkey, a dog, a guinea pig for our benefit. We would find other ways to heal our wounds, heal our bodies. But the healing of the mind is something totally different. That healing gradually takes place if you are with nature, with that orange on the tree, and the blade of grass that pushes through cement, and the hills covered, hidden, by the clouds."[250]

XI. Realization

Krishnamurti was no epistomologist. Krishnamurti was a mystic. However, particularly during the last years of his life, the mystic tried to clad the path to true understanding in words which he regarded as comprehendable. As happened in other fields as well, he made the mistake of believing that this would be possible for 'everybody.' Krishnamurti did not regard intelligence as a special gift but as the potential of each and every individual.[251] Again, he did not take into account the evolutionary factor and so he totally neglected the idea of a comprehension that can only develop gradually. The reason for this is found in his understanding of time. Realization, true cognition, stands independent of stored knowledge. "As long as there is a perceiver in the past, what he perceives is not the truth. First comes experience; then experience breeds knowledge; and that knowledge is limited, whether it is in the past, present, or future."[252] Only in freedom from time, at the onset of another dimension, can the touch of REALITY take place. Here Krishnamurti approaches German mysticism as it appears, for example, in the idea of the 'ewigen nu' (the eternal now) of Meister Eckhart. For Krishnamurti, too, the key is to be found in the 'now.' "To see what is without yesterday, is the now."[253]

To convey this idea was not always easy for Krishnamurti. An example of his difficulty here can be seen in a conversation he had with David Bohm concerning the dissolution of the Order of the Star, during which Krishnamurti tried to make clear that his decision was made because of an 'insight' and not through thought.[254] In Krishnamurti's view, thoughts were only able to describe the outside of reality but never its true nature. "*Insight* has nothing to do with thought. If insight is the product of thought, then that insight is partial.... We can never have it (omniscience, P.M.). Thought can never capture it. We might be an astrophysicist and investigate the universe, but the understanding will be always within the field of thought. So the universe can often be captured by thought. We can understand it logically, we can understand what it is made of—gases and so on. But that's not *universe*."[255]

Krishnamurti's answer to the hermeneutic question was that truth and method exclude one another. Truth can only be found through the insight of the individual and such insight cannot be gained on often-traveled paths or through particular methods. Therefore Krishnamurti also disapproved of psychoanalysis. The human being has to learn to understand himself, "but not according to Freud, Jung, and the psychologists and analysts, that is too infantile, for if I learn according to them I learn what they are, I am not learning about myself."[256] The answer in the field of epistemology, as in the social-political field, is again individual responsibility. Neither following certain political advice nor the use of epistemological methods can help. For Krishnamurti, it was important to develop an openness for access to the inner reality—which was synonymous with intelligence and love in his view. There the 'key to cognition' was hidden. "When there is the discovery of the cause there is that supreme intelligence, which in its very nature is compassionate love."[257]

Spirit and Mind

The only thing a computer cannot do
—compared to a human being—
is to look into the evening sky.

The idea of spirit in Krishnamurti's talks and books cannot always be determined precisely. Frequently he used the term 'mind' which he also takes to refer to consciousness or reasoning. When he talks about spirit in the deep sense, he refers to a cosmic reality, in the sense of an 'Omnipresence' (All-Geist) whom he regarded as universal.[258] This spirit was beyond the brain, was not even connected to it, though was able to use it.[259]

Krishnamurti also differentiated the spirit from the western concept of psyche and soul which he believed is equivalent to the brain.[260] During a conversation with Asit Chandmal, Krishnamurti tried to state more precisely his understanding of spirit, intelligence and brain. "When the brain is silent, the mind operates. That is the intelligence of the universe.... An insight into the operation of limitation frees the brain from limitation. Insight can only arise when there is no memory, and so no time. When the whole brain is operating, it has no direction. It is free of the past. Insight is mind operating on brain."[261] Most remarkably, Krishnamurti even builds a bridge from intelligence, by way of intuition, to inspiration. "Intuition is the highest point of intelligence and to me keeping alive that intelligence is inspiration."[262] Here, his concept of insight comes close to traditional western philosophy where cognition is connected with inspiration. If one draws a line from one level to the other, alertness leads to intelligence, intelligence via intuition to inspiration; and the vehicle that carries the seeking mind on this path—is love.

Truth

The moment, one follows somebody,
one stops following the truth.

Krishnamurti answered the central human quest for truth in the light of his dynamic world view: "Truth has no path, and that is the beauty of truth, it is living."[263] Another time he is even more precise, bringing into play the aspect of compassion, one could call it even love for all creation: "...truth has no path. There is no path. When one has compassion, with its intelligence, one will come upon that which is eternally true."[264]

Truth is a central word for Krishnamurti and is coupled closely to beauty, freedom, and love. Truth had to be ever-new, had to be free from the burden of the past, free from the burden of memory. Truth, at the same time, was alertness, clear and unprejudiced observation of the outer and the inner life.

There is a short story that Krishnamurti often told, wound around the legend of the Buddha as was often the case, which sheds significant light on Krishnamurti's idea of truth. "I meet the Buddha. I have listened to him very deeply. In me the whole truth of what he says is abiding, and he goes away. He has told me very carefully, 'Be a light to yourself.' The seed is flowering. I may miss him. He was a friend, somebody whom I really loved. However, what is really important is that seed of truth which he has planted—by my alertness, awareness, intense listening, that seed will flower.

Otherwise, what is the point of somebody having it? If X has this extraordinary illumination, a sense of immensity, compassion, and all that, if only he has it and he dies, what is the point of it all? What?"[265]

With this story, Krishnamurti does not tell the story of Buddha and his disciples, he tells the story of Krishnamurti and his disciples. In addition, it expresses in a poetic form his hope that he might be understood beyond the outer meaning of his words. With the last five sentences of his talk in Washington, on April 21, 1985, he summarized what he said in this story. He who watches this talk on video will pick up a feeling for the depth and the charisma passing from Krishnamurti to his listeners.

"The brain is extraordinarily capable, has infinite capacity, but we have made it so small and petty.

"So when there is that space and emptiness and therefore immense energy—energy is passion, love and compassion and intelligence—then there is that truth which is most holy, most sacred, that which man has sought from time immemorial. That truth doesn't lie in any temple, in any mosque, in any church. And it has no path to it except through one's own understanding of oneself, inquiring, studying, learning. Then there is that which is eternal."[266]

XII. Evolution

The really important thing is this knowledge—
the knowledge of God's plan for men.
For God has a plan and that plan is evolution.
—Alcyone—

A few years before his death and during an interview with the *New York Times*, Paul L. Montgomery asked Krishnamurti whether he believed his teachings had changed anything in the life of humanity. He answered: "A little, sir. But not much."[267] This simple remark is more significant than one might think in helping to understand a basic problem. It represents Krishnamurti's self-assessment—perhaps with resignation—that evolution is measured in different rhythms of time than he had assumed.

This misassessment illustrates two points: On the one hand, Krishnamurti, with his extraordinary modesty, may not have realized, how big the gap was between himself and a 'normal person;' on the other hand, it clarifies how dramatically Krishnamurti was wrong in his belief that illumination and breakthrough to reality—the exact wording being unimportant at that point—could be realized by everybody *here and now*. Geoffrey Hodson had accused him of this misconception earlier,[268] it nearly prevented the publication of his *Notebook*,[269] and with prophetic premonition Emily Lutyens had hinted at these dangers in a letter she wrote to him in the thirties. "You seem surprised that people do not understand you but I should be far more surprised if they did! After all, you are upsetting everything in which they have ever believed—knocking out their foundations and putting in its place a nebulous abstraction. You speak of what you yourself say is indescribable—and not to be understood till discovered for oneself. How then do you expect them to understand? You are speaking from another dimension and have quite forgotten what it is like to live in a world of three dimensions.... You are advocating a complete destruction of the ego in order to achieve something about which you can know nothing until you achieve it! Naturally people prefer their egos of which they do know something.... No human problem means anything to you because you are ego-less and your abstraction of bliss means nothing to people who are still desirous to live in the world as they know it."[270] Why, particularly in the second half of his life, did Krishnamurti refuse to accept spiritual evolution? Why did he reject the notion of any kind of maturing process, what G. Hodson referred to as 'the development of the inner life,' and that it is a cosmic law that cannot willingly be switched on and off? Was acknowledgment of the idea of evolution a block on the path to inner insight?

"I can never be finished...." Krishnamurti wrote to Emily Lutyens in 1931.[271] At this time he was still taking evolution into account which included spiritual growth as well. Three years earlier, still in the days of the Order of the Star, the traditional world view of theosophy was discernible in his talks, though with a remarkable new emphasis. In his Ommen talks in 1927, Krishnamurti outlined the theosophical cosmogony, according to which individual life sparks emerge from the Omnipresence to struggle on long paths of evolution for perfection. He uses a myth from the creation of the world for his story and continues: "Little by little that person whom you know as Krishnamurti, who started as a separate spark, as a separate being from the flame, has been able, through great experiences, to be unified with the flame.

"I have told you that story, because ordinarily, when an individual starts as a separate being, it takes eons, it takes centuries of time to acquire all the lessons, all the teachings that life can give before there is the possibility of perceiving, of seeing that vision of Liberation and Happiness, because you are now in the presence of the Beloved, and when the Beloved is with you, time as such ceases. You need to go through all the experiences of sorrow, of affliction, of grief, of intense joy, to perceive that goal which is the end for all."[272]

I believe this early statement is an important key to the understanding of his rejection of the idea of evolution. Apparently, Krishnamurti thought it possible, or even likely, that the divine power that revealed itself through him could lead to a spontaneous transformation. (During the years 1910 and 1925 there had been many occurrences that supported this belief.) Otherwise, I cannot make sense of some of his statements and some of his actions.

Krishnamurti's statements about the idea of evolution are contradictory from the very beginning, as can be seen in a thorough study of his Early Writings. In Ojai in 1930, he responded to a questioner as follows: "Evolution is an undeniable fact."[273] In 1928 he had confessed that many of his insights "grew in me unconsciously."[274] Therefore he admitted an inner process of maturing. One year earlier, in Eerde, he had clarified for the first time—contradicting theosophical beliefs—that "one can, at any stage of evolution, wherever one may be, attain Liberation."[275] However, some of his attempts to explain a practical realization of this idea are almost touchingly naive, for example when he tries to explain how he would convey the idea of freedom to a child.[276] At the same venue in 1929, he spoke about the idea that illumination would not appear out of the blue but that it is a "continuous process."[277] When E. A. Wodehouse mentioned in one of their discussions that some of his statements about evolution were difficult to understand, he stated his thoughts more precisely. "On the other hand, it may be true—probably it is—that a certain amount of evolutionary growth will be necessary before anybody will have a real wish in him to make this ego-annihilation effort. The statement, therefore, that liberation can be reached at *any* stage should be modified.... From this point of view the whole journey towards liberation (if one can put it so) is one long liberation. The great thing is to be facing in the right direction. After that, the length of time which the journey may take does not matter. To have 'begun liberating' is what counts."[278] This more differentiated point of view seems to have expressed Krishnamurti's opinion for several years, for Carlo Suares quotes him in the 1950 edition of his book: "So, there can be an evolution, the inward continuous renewal, only when you understand yourself."[279] Here, evolution is linked to consciousness, but the question remains open as to how evolution takes place *before* it reaches that level on which self-realization occurs.[280] The question is amplified even further when one reads a sentence by Krishnamurti taken from a dialog with David Bohm: "I don't think there is psychological evolution at all."[281] Even more directly, Krishnamurti states in his *Journal*: "As we were saying, there is no psychological evolution. The psyche can never become or grow into something which it is not. Conceit and arrogance cannot grow into better and more conceit, nor can selfishness, which is the common lot of all human beings, become more and more selfish, more and more of its own nature."[282] While reading these words, I always ask myself in what way Krishnamurti really wanted certain words, like psyche, for example, to be understood. Clearly he rejected the word psyche as a term for the true inner being of man because "the brain...has created the psyche."[283] And Krishnamurti did not see the brain as an individual organ with which one can express oneself (according to karmic structures) but as a result of the entire evolutionary process. It was "not *my* brain; not *my* thinking. It is *thinking*."[284] Although this idea fundamentally contradicts one of Krishnamurti's experiences which he describes in his *Notebook* on July 20, 1961.

Subsequent to a mystical touch by a divine reality, he notes: "All this seemed to affect the brain; it was not as it was before."[285] Here a definite evolutionary element is apparent and it seems indisputable that a brain like Krishnamurti's was necessary to manifest this experience in a material world. Only a soul that had matured to perfection over millennia would be able to experience this transformation, though it remains indisputable that this experience, to use Krishnamurti's wording, is open to "all thinking." Should Sheldrake's theory of Morphogenetic Fields prove correct, it could work as a scientific model.[285a]

During the last ten years of his life, Krishnamurti must have realized that his ideas about immediate transformation, without any form of evolutionary process, could not be correct in that form. Discussions with friends and disciples who confessed their inability to make a transition, with its radical suddenness in Krishnamurti's sense, set him thinking.[286] An event in the Rishi Valley School that was documented by Mary Lutyens illustrates this fact. "On 21 September K asked at a staff meeting: 'How do you instantly, without time, make the students see that self-interest is the root of conflict? Not only see it but instantly be transformed?'

He went on to say that of all the hundreds of students who had passed through Rishi Valley, his oldest school, not one had been changed. After the meeting, when they were alone, Mary asked him what was the point of having students if none of them in all those years had been changed? If, with all his influence, no student had been transformed, how could the rest of us, who had apparently not changed either, bring about change in the students? 'If you haven't done it, is there any likelihood that we can?' she asked. 'I don't know,' he replied, but he said this rather jokingly, evidently not wanting to continue with a serious subject."[287] Obviously, after all those years of traveling and teaching Krishnamurti realized that even he himself was not able to do more than plant a seed, a seed that would start developing and which would eventually flower. [288]

Pupul Jayakar must have experienced Krishnamurti in a similar way in his later years. "On a walk, he said, 'the inquiry within is infinite. You must be alone, stripped, then you can take a journey into the unknown.' He was still probing, feeling out, he continued to question."[289] Similar to the experience of other great sages, we find this strange contradiction of 'completed' unification and unending progress for Krishnamurti as well. Perhaps it is only resolved for somebody who sees from 'face to face' himself—but everybody needs to mature, before the inner eyes begin to see.

XIII. Fear

Before investigating Krishnamurti's thoughts about fear and how to overcome it, it seems instructive to me to look into two examples from his personal experiences which are closely connected to this problem.

As a child, Krishnamurti was most likely quite timid, a characteristic which C. W. Leadbeater soon noticed. It was a goal of Leadbeater's educational method to help his disciples overcome fear. One day Leadbeater observed that while Krishnamurti was swimming he tried to avoid a certain deep spot in the bay of Adyar. Krishnamurti had not seen Leadbeater watching him and so he was shocked when Leadbeater said to him in the evening: "Let's go again to the sea to look for a very deep spot." Confronted with his fear, Krishnamurti succeeded in overcoming it. This remained a deep and lasting experience for him. His experience was to confront his fear directly and to overcome it in doing so. This idea became a central theme in his later teachings.[290]

The second event points to a deeper dimension and touches a topic of great importance—the encounter with the 'evil.' Krishnamurti was no follower of naive devil or satanic ideas, etc.; but he knew of the reality of demonic forces. He had touched the source of the good, but he also knew about the forces of destruction. "K said, 'Fear attracts evil. To talk about evil is to invite it.' Suddenly, Krishnaji became strange and far removed. He drew his arms close to himself, drawing his body into the smallest possible space. Then he said, 'Do you feel it in the room?' His face had changed. The room was charged with power. Then K said, 'Before we sleep, I will have to dispel it. Protect this place.' He would not say what he would do, but something had to be done. A little later he got up and walked round, circumambulating each of the rooms.... A little later, Krishnaji came back to the dining room. He was serene, his face beautiful, his eyes limpid. The atmosphere had totally changed. Whatever was there had been totally wiped away.

"Over the years Nandini and I had often talked of Krishnaji's attitude to good and evil. He had told us, 'Evil is a fact. Leave it alone. Your mind should not play with evil. Thinking about it is to invite it. Hatred, jealousy, attract evil. That is why it is important for the mind and body to be still and silent and not let any strong emotions arise, without watching relentlessly. Deterioration walks one step behind you. No matter who you are.'"[291] His immense spiritual power and the mighty protection that surrounded him always made it possible for Krishnamurti to dispel the darkness with his light. However, he was watching constantly to sense a nearing of the shadows.

Fear closed the door to the light and Krishnamurti believed that the fear of death was the central fear. In early years he had already tried to point out how this fear could be overcome by experiencing a transcendental reality. He did not give the traditional answers about life after death, which he regarded as a poor, sometimes even paralyzing, consolation. For him, the dynamic of life did not express itself in a consoling certainty of life after death but in the realization of a true immortality. This step, from an esoteric teaching of the other side to a rational appeal to self-realization, was quite difficult for many of his friends, including Emily Lutyens. She was not able to correlate Krishnamurti's development from one who only a short time before had sympathetically met his late brother with the Krishnamurti of a "radically new reality."[292] Did Krishnamurti again expect too much of his listeners? Was it not necessary to find a satisfactory answer to the fear of death, the fear of the void, first, without losing the real goal?[293]

Death was the ending of time, the ending of life. Time was a helper of fear. To overcome fear meant to overcome time. Krishnamurti dedicated one of his talks in the Saanen meeting in 1975 to the topic of fear and especially to the connection he had found between fear and time. "If one is to be free of fear, one must be free of time. If there were no time one would have no fear. I wonder if you see that? If there were no tomorrow, only the now, fear, as a movement of thought, ends. If there is complete psychological security there is no fear."[294] Time and thought are the roots of fear. A good job today, layed off tomorrow. A healthy body today, disease tomorrow. Fear of change to the negative, determined significantly by thought. Again, Krishnamurti's advice was to turn from time to timelessness, from the transitory to reality. But what happened to all those who were unable to take this big step, those who were left with fear? Intellectual insight into a fear that was determined by time and thought did not overcome it nor cut its deep roots. This helplessness is impressively apparent in Pupul Jayakar's report of a meeting with Krishnamurti's Indian friends. Fear became physical, concrete, and nobody was able to propose a practical solution. Only sinking into a deep silence—probably initiated by Krishnamurti—opened an inner door to transform the fear. According to Pupul Jayakar, the event ended as follows: "I had listened. I came away seeing that freedom from fear was not in any action from within or without, but could only be when the brain was totally still.

135

The quietness generated by dialog remained with me, and I slept that night without fear. Cataclysmic, primeval fears have not arisen within me since that dialog. The few fears that have arisen have been at the surface level of consciousness and so possible to deal with.

"In the days that followed K was to speak to me of the nature of loneliness. It was an extraordinary state of being, completely isolated. It was the essence of the self—the 'me' with its web of words in which the mind is caught. He asked me to face complete inward loneliness; only in that was there freedom from fear.

"'To be free of fear is to be free of time,' he said. I received those words and held them close."[295]

Fear cannot be overcome on its own terms and a direct battle actually strengthens it. The power to overcome it successfully lies on another dimension. An immense energy is to be found there if one can let go of the old patterns and find a new, non-predetermined attitude, an attitude that can be characterized as innocent purity. And "only out of innocence can you solve problems, and innocence is a mind that is meeting everything anew."[296]

Krishnamurti frequently elaborated on two aspects of fear—striving for success and recognition, and the lack of freedom it brings. "As long as success is our goal we cannot be rid of fear, for the desire to succeed inevitably breeds the fear of failure. That is why the young should not be taught to worship success."[297] The compulsive striving for superiority or even equality with others creates a tremendous amount of fear, ranging from simple feelings of inferiority to absolute angst. To allocate one's own worth in comparison to others or through others inevitably leads to fear and overlooks the nature of existence.[298] In Krishnamurti's view, this socially induced fear could only be resolved in the long run by breaking the molds that existed in the schools. Conformity, imitation and adaptation all had to be given up to help the true nature of an individual unfold without fear.[299] The key to this was inner freedom. In particular, this included the removal of any bond to self-established authority. "One of the results of fear is the acceptance of authority in human affairs. Authority is created by our desire to be right, to be secure, to be comfortable, to have no conscious conflicts or disturbances; but nothing which results from fear can help us to understand our problems, even though fear may take the form of respect and submission to the so-called wise. The wise wield no authority, and those in authority are not wise. Fear in whatever form prevents the understanding of ourselves and of our relationship to all things."[300] This step required an alert analysis of society, its morals and its constraints. For this task, an extraordinary intelligence was necessary, a spiritual intelligence which, in Krishnamurti's view, was characterized by love, kindness and compassion. This intelligence provided the energy needed to become free of all fear; for freedom was an absolute necessity. Nobody who had fear could ever be free.[301] However, this freedom could be found far more easily on the mountain tops of the spirit than could be realized on the plains of searching souls. Many human fears were rooted deeply, coming from long ago, and to overcome them required immense power—and not all of those souls Krishnamurti tried to help were able to keep their eyes on such fear without lowering their gaze.

XIV. Freedom

*Freedom means leaving traditions behind
and experimenting.*

The idea of freedom touches the very heart of Krishnamurti's teachings. The boy Krishna was already searching for freedom in the framework of his theosophical education; and the Krishnamurti of the twenties was shaped deeply by the effort to gain spiritual freedom and independence that culminated in the dissolving of the Order of the Star.

In his view, the idea of freedom was the essence of the nature of humanity. "Complete freedom is the only important thing in human life."[302] However, freedom must not be interpreted as a banal expression of arbitrariness or lack of restraint. For Krishnamurti, freedom was not only a unique value, but also a unique virtue. "Freedom requires a great deal of discipline. Freedom implies great humility, innate inward discipline and work."[303] This statement helps clarify which quality distinguished freedom in Krishnamurti's sense. It is the freedom of the purified consciousness, which has freed itself from personal wishes and desires, and has risen to the clarity of the experience of unity in which inner and outer freedom are one.

Krishnamurti affirmed the outer becoming free—for himself and others—in a unique way during his shattering talk on August 2, 1929, when he dissolved the Order of the Star in Ommen. At both the beginning and at the end of the talk, one finds the remarkable words: "I maintain that Truth is a pathless land, and you cannot approach it by any path whatsoever, by any religion, by any sect. That is my point of view and I adhere to that absolutely and unconditionally.... If you first understand that, then you will see how impossible it is to organize a belief. A belief is purely an individual matter, and you cannot and must not organize it. If you do, it becomes dead, crystallized; it becomes a creed, a sect, a religion, to be imposed on others....

"No Man from outside can make you free; nor can organized worship, nor the immolation of yourselves for a cause, make you free; nor can forming yourselves into an organization, nor throwing yourselves into work, make you free. You use a typewriter to write letters, but you do not put it on an altar and worship it."[304] For many, those words and the event itself came as a surprise; but they had not listened carefully to Krishnamurti's words, had not paid enough attention to his writings. Otherwise, in one of his early poetic works they would have been able to detect a sketch of that which would later burst out so spectacularly. In *The Search* Krishnamurti writes:

The Happiness that knows
Of no loneliness,
Of immense certainty,
Of detachment,
Of love that is free of persons,
That is free from prejudices,
That is not bound by tradition,
That is not bound by authority,
That is not bound by superstitions,
That is of no religion.
The Happiness
That is not at the command of another,
That is of no priest,

That is of no sect,
That requires no labels,
That is bound by no law,... [305]

In fact, all later calls for freedom are preconceived in these words—his calls towards religions and sects, for example. "It is the division which denies freedom and love, not organization. When organization divides, it leads to war. Belief in any form, ideals, however noble or effective, breed division. Organized religion is the cause of division, just like nationality and power groups." [306]

Also, the statement he made twenty-five years later is in essence a footnote to that early confession: "We are all slaves to tradition and we think we are also totally different from each other. We are not. We go through the same great miseries, unhappiness, shed tears, we are all human beings, not Hindus, Muslims, or Russians—those are all labels without meaning. The mind must be totally free; which means that one has to stand completely alone; and we are so frightened to stand alone.

"The mind must be free, utterly still, not controlled. When the mind is completely religious it is not only free but capable of inquiring into the nature of truth to which there is no guide, no path. It is only the silent mind, the mind that is free, that can come upon that which is beyond time." [307] His words have the greater precision and depth of a mature personality but they still emerge from that clarity of earlier years.

I consider authority as my last example: "No system, outwardly, is going to help man. On the contrary, systems are going to divide people, that is what has always been happening in the world. And inwardly, to accept another as your authority, to accept the authority of a system, is to live in isolation, in separateness, therefore there is no freedom." [308]

Freedom from tradition, authority, religion, sects and personality cult, all central topics for Krishnamurti in the sixty years after 1926—and all of them already entirely present and ripe in the young man of the twenties. In my view, this continuity is not regarded highly enough. The Krishnamurti of the seventies was not more critical of religion and authority than the Krishnamurti of the year 1926. The young Krishnamurti had already detached himself from outer limitations and from religious groups; then when—for him—the perversion of the Holy occurred (Huizen 1925), he put religion *in the denominational sense*, no matter which one, in the category of a lack of freedom. Only the religion of the heart, which develops in freedom and love, in true humility and compassion, complied with his idea of religion. Freedom could not be the end, the promise of a certain religious salvation, but had to determine the beginning, the middle and the end of the path. "If the end is freedom, the beginning must be free, for the end and the beginning are one. There can be self-knowledge and intelligence only when there is freedom at the very outset; and freedom is denied by the acceptance of authority."[309] It will surprise nobody that orthodox communities, from the Roman Catholic clergy to the high-cast Brahman hierarchy, saw in him a dangerous demagogue. His endeavor to set human beings *absolutely and unconditionally* free robbed those people of any form of influence and power. The free human no longer had any need for a priestly mediator, to 'reconcile' with the absolute spirit. One who had found inner freedom finds outer freedom without much difficulty as well. Krishnamurti found a deep meaning even in the opposite idea: "Independence without freedom is meaningless. If you have freedom you don't need independence."[310]

During his dialog with the sannyasins in Srinagar, Krishnamurti pointed out these connections in particularly strong terms: "Putting on a saffron robe does not mean renouncing. You can never renounce the world, because the world is part of you. You renounce a few cows, a house, but to renounce your heredity, your tradition, the burden of your condition, that demands enormous inquiry."[311] Repeatedly Krishnamurti talked about the dangers associated with walking well-trodden paths and clinging to old patterns without seeing their limitations. Only through alert observation of these old patterns could one prevent the paralysis and decrepitude of the mind, though he did not differentiate between old patterns, whether they be three thousand or only thirty years old. "If however you would be free of violence, which is buried so deep, you must first learn about yourself. You can only learn if you observe yourself—not according to Jung or Freud or some other specialist—then you are merely learning what they have already told you, so that is not learning at all. If you really want to learn about yourself, then you must put away all the comforting authority of others, and observe."[312] Again, a greater affinity with Buddhist rather than with Christian ideas is apparent in his criticism of authority and religion. It is not belief that leads to bliss, but doubts that lead you towards your goal. "Because it is only through doubt that you come to the Brahman, not through acceptance of authority."[313] This is not a preconception by Krishnamurti, but a certain preference; and of course, in the same light, he too must be questioned, whether his exclusion of belief and his approval of doubt is a limitation in and of itself.

In this context, I refer to an answer Krishnamurti gave to a question in 1947 about surrendering to the will of God. It provides a convincing clarification of his idea of freedom in contrast to religious dependency. "Surrendering to the will of God implies that you already know the will of God. You are not surrendering to something you do not know. If you know Reality, you cannot surrender to it. You cease to exist. There is no surrendering to a higher will. If you are surrendering to a higher will then that higher will is the projection of yourself, for the Real cannot be known through the known. It comes into being only when the known ceases to be."[314] The radical approach of a Taoist (The Tao that I can talk about is not the Tao) or of a medieval Christian mystic (The God I can name is not the true God) come to mind; but the number of like-minded spirits with a similar deep religiousness is small.

For Krishnamurti, freedom was an absolute value, a solitary, sacrosanct object. If at all he had a second constant next to this central ideal of his life—then it was Love. Love and Freedom, if they were true in Krishnamurti's strict sense, complemented one another, they were even inseparable in their true meaning. "And when there is freedom, there is energy; and when there is freedom it can never do anything wrong. Freedom is entirely different from revolt. There is no such thing as doing right or wrong when there is freedom. You *are* free and from that center you act. And hence there is no fear, and a mind that has no fear is capable of great love. And when there is love it can do what it will."[315] A person who is truly loving can do whatever he wants because the true loving human *always* acts according to the wisdom of God. Such a person cannot abuse this freedom, living in and through love. Love is the guarantor for true action. The loving person will always be an invincible fighter for freedom and the one who has gained inner freedom will always be a shining messenger of love.

Freedom and Love—Krishnamurti's entire life, as well as every one of his words, are embedded in them. Freedom and Love—they are the key to understanding the mystery of Jiddu Krishnamurti.

XV. Love

Love does not know about yesterday and tomorrow;
it is always new....

If freedom is the door to the understanding of Krishnamurti, love is the nature, the essence that awaits those who pass through it. If there was ever anything that forced his critics to concede a connection to the Christ, it was the unbounded love that emerged from him and which everyone who was open to his true message was able to feel. This all-embracing love for humanity appeared on countless documented and undocumented occasions. From the beggars, to whom he gave many presents as a young boy, to burglars, whom he followed in the middle of the night to warn about the police, to the many simple people in the dirty streets of India and the countless seekers who sat at his feet for nearly three quarters of a century. All of them met an illumined being who, in his own way, revealed divine love. Often those who only know Krishnamurti from his writings do not see this central aspect of his being. They did not know him and in most cases they do not know those whose hearts he touched.

At the beginning of this book I mentioned my own touch by Krishnamurti and I will highlight the experiences of two other people who knew Krishnamurti very well in his early and late years respectively. During the Spring of 1991 I spent some inspiring days at Brockwood Park as I supplemented the source material for this book. During those days I had many personal talks with both students and teachers at the school, including its head, Scott Forbes, who was with Krishnamurti during his last hours. I was deeply moved by the words and recollections of Forbes, which showed me that this man had been transformed by Krishnamurti's love in the depths of his heart and how this transformation was still molding him and emanating from him. Scott Forbes was, and remains, one of the many living examples of the transformation in and through love that were induced by Krishnamurti.

The second episode touches a totally different aspect. It became clear to me during a conversation about Krishnamurti with Dora Kunz when, along with many interesting details and descriptions of events from the early years of Krishnamurti, one particular remark she made stuck in my head. She suggested that the Krishnamurti of the late twenties suppressed, or even 'switched off' a part of his spiritual abilities because his extraordinary sensibility and his indescribable compassion almost resulted in a total breakdown. In particular, the immense misery in India, which causes great emotional torment for even a person of normal compassion, was nearly unbearable for the young Krishnamurti. Therefore, his extended perceptive faculty was, in light of his loving heart, an unendurable torture. His emotional pains threatened to crush his heart and therefore he had to protect himself. Who can imagine the pains of the great teachers of humanity concerning the misery and the aberrations of their brothers and sisters? How many 'bloody tears' may they have shed in the face of the hatred and the violence they saw on earth?

One has to read Krishnamurti's description of his vow to the Masters and the Lord of the World—notwithstanding the question of the significance of the Masters—to understand what this promise, "to make your life all love,"[316]

146

meant to him. He wanted to serve this love with all his might, wanted to be an ambassador of the love of the infinite spirit.

Sometimes he hinted about this mission, during healing sessions for example, but for the most part he did not talk about it in public. "You know I have had this healing power, or whatever it is, since my childhood. I rarely exercise it. But this time there was an urge to help. Of course Love has played the major part in this healing. You know what I mean—Don't you?"[317] When he felt that he was understood, when he felt he could talk from heart to heart, he dropped the veil to his personality a little bit and let the light shine through in its abundance. In his view, most of the time people were not open enough to really understand him. He saw one reason for this in the loss of their connection to nature. "To be alone. To have a quality of love about a tree, protective and yet alone. We are losing the feeling for trees, and so we are losing love for man. When we can't love nature, we can't love man."[318] When he was asked how one could open oneself to love, he referred to nature as the first step. Also, his advice to the teachers of his schools—that it would be more important for the children to understand the falling of a leaf than to recall intellectual theories—heads in that same direction. Loving care for creation opened the path to the inner; and this love at the same time was a powerful protection, because "when there is love there is protection. Hatred permits evil to enter."[319]

In modern society, with all its order directed to functionality and violence, he saw an enormous lack of the ability to love. Therefore, his social criticism could be harsh. "If you really loved your children, would you educate them in the way you do, train them, force them to conform to the established order of a rotten society? If you really loved your children, would you allow them to be killed or horribly mutilated

147

in a war, whether it be your war or somebody else's? If you observe all this, it indicates, does it not, that there is no love at all?"[320] His analysis of social conditions lead him to a decisive rejection of all ideologies and 'isms.' Real change could only be carried out from the inside, but political changes only remained on the surface. Krishnamurti wanted a 'revolution of love.' "It is only love that brings about this total action and that can possibly bring about this complete sense of unity."[321] This love Krishnamurti talked about was the "truth that sets you free." It was a transcendental love that came from an inner touch by an absolute reality. This anchoring in the divine being must always be taken into account when one reads particularly radical sentences like those in his *Notebook*, in which he wrote on November 29, 1961: "To go beyond thought is virtue and that virtue is heightened sensitivity which is love. Love and there is no sin; love and do what you will and then there is no sorrow."[322]

From time to time Krishnamurti was asked whether he would love one person more or less than another. He always said he would not, referring to the all-encompassing love that did not have a personal component. "You ask me just now about personal love, and my answer is that I no longer know it. Personal love does not exist for me. Love is for me a constant inner state.... I have the same feeling of affection for all and each of you."[323] Krishnamurti expressed this form of love in two brief but poetic statements, in 1930 in Ommen and in 1931 in Adyar, which Emily Lutyens has passed on to us. "Pure love is like the perfume of the rose, given to all. The sun does not care on whom it shines.... The quality of true love, of pure love, knows no such distinctions as wife and husband, son, father, mother."[324]

Krishnamurti regarded his private life as his own personal affair, especially where women were concerned. He should have known from his own experiences that this atmosphere of privacy could not be maintained permanently. It is not surprising, therefore, that this aspect of his life was also dragged into public view. I doubt that the preservation of his image as a pure saint was the reason that Krishnamurti did not talk about his intimate relationships, as is implied by Radha Sloss. Rather, his own bashfulness and the respect he showed for the private lives of those close to him, played a part. Krishnamurti never characterized sexuality *in itself* as something negative or as something that one must overcome. It was *one* aspect of the life of people; but it should be seen in the right context. How difficult that was, he had to realize by the fact that his relationships were always only answered on the level the other one was on. He was confronted with a range of such problems in his private life but they did not dominate his life in the way the Sloss biography, which focuses on this subject, leads her readers to believe. Krishnamurti passed through all aspects of being human, from the level of personal love to the mountain tops from which one can touch the absolute spirit. This is possibly a sign of encouragement for those who might otherwise shrink back from the immense task of emulating the great teachers of humanity, when sometimes the path seems too steep.

For Krishnamurti the extraordinary social problem of sexuality was its coldness and lack of love. "When you are in love, vulnerable, sex is not a problem."[325] But those qualities were rare. In Krishnamurti's view, sexuality degenerated into an outlet for lust, to replace missing creativity and lack of divine intelligence—a task sexuality is not able to perform. In 1976 Krishnamurti talked to the young professional Rajesh Dal, who had many problems caused by his suppressed sexuality. With great empathy, Krishnamurti tried to show him the middle path, between aimless lust and tormenting asceticism.

"Sex is like a tender flower, an intense flame, delicate and rare. It has to be nurtured and cherished. You have to be specially watchful when it is not operating as nature intended. To let sex function freely is to dissipate energy; to suppress it brutally is to destroy something delicate and intensely beautiful. So watch it with warmth, nurture it, let it discover itself and unfold—neither denying it nor succumbing to it."[326] The intimate relationship between two people, which in its ideal form is the connection of two souls, could create an opening for Divine Love, something from which he believed most of his fellow humans were far removed. In a letter he wrote to Padmabai, an Indian companion, he expresses his deep feelings: "You have no idea of the joy of true impersonal love."[327] Krishnamurti was confronted repeatedly with feelings of helplessness at his inability to communicate his understanding of love. One reason for this may be that for him "love was beyond the brain."[328] Because of that, it was beyond intellectual mediation. In addition, it could not be reached by rites, methods or disciplines. "The monk, the priest, the sanyasi torture their bodies and their character in their longing for this but it evades them. For it cannot be bought; neither sacrifice, virtue nor prayer can bring this love."[329] First, the I, the person, the limited and small human being had to learn to step aside and to let God be active. "So God, or whatever name you give it, is when *you* are not. When you are, it is not. When you are not, love is. When you are, love is not."[330] This non-existence seemed to be difficult to explain. It was beyond the familiar frame. In one of his most beautiful discourses on love, published in *Freedom from the Known*, Krishnamurti tries with intensity to reveal the mystery of love in daily life.

"Don't you know what it means really to love somebody—to love without hate, without jealousy, without anger, without wanting to interfere with what he is doing or thinking, without condemning, without comparing—don't you know what it means? Where there is love is there comparison? When you love someone with all your heart, with all your mind, with all your body, with your entire being, is there comparison? When you totally abandon yourself to that love there is not the other.

"Does love have responsibility and duty, and will it use those words? When you do something out of duty is there any love in it? In duty there is no love. The structure of duty in which the human being is caught is destroying him. So long as you are compelled to do something because it is your duty you don't love what you are doing. When there is love there is no duty and no responsibility."[331]

Krishnamurti was often asked why, for decades, he had taken so much trouble to travel and give his talks while society seemed to be frozen in its inability to love and his words echoed unheard. One of the answers he gave, only a few years before his death, unveils the beauty of his great soul, the beauty of a vast love: "I think when one sees something true and beautiful one wants to tell people about it, out of affection, out of compassion, out of love. And if there are those who are not interested that is all right. Can you ask the flower why it grows, why it has perfume? It is for the same reason that the speaker talks."[332]

Krishnamurti was unable to express the mystery of love with words. However, he was able to touch those who were open to his touch, like the lotus, still covered by the dew, opens to the first rays of the sun at dawn. More was not possible for him. Therefore, I will not even try to continue where Krishnamurti's abilities ended. However, it may be possible to weave a tapestry of flowers and so help the reader to approach the mystery in meditative silence. In this light,

151

some of Krishnamurti's deepest words on the subject of love close this chapter, to begin a new chapter in the heart.

Compassion means passion for all; love does not suffer. [333]

To love is the greatest thing of all, for in it there has to be the complete abandonment of oneself. [334]

The goal of human feeling is love which is complete in itself, utterly detached, knowing neither subject nor object, a love which gives equally to all without demanding anything whatever in return, a love which is its own eternity.[335]

So love is something that cannot be invited or cultivated. It comes about naturally, easily, when the other things are not. And in learning about oneself one comes upon this: where there is love, there is compassion; and compassion has its own intelligence. That is the supreme form of intelligence, not the intelligence of thought, intelligence of cunning, deceptions and all the rest of it. It's only when there is complete love and compassion that there is that excellence of intelligence which is not mechanical. [336]

To love is to be aware of eternity.[337]

XVI. Mysticism

Krishnamurti is given the titles philosopher, teacher of wisdom, sometimes even agnostic or atheist—but from his true being Krishnamurti was a mystic. His theme was the unity of all being, a unity built upon freedom and love; and this unity extended from rocks in the mountains to the light of the Infinite Divine Being. For Krishnamurti, all being was filled with the hidden holiness of the Divine and to reveal that perfection was his life goal. His being, striving for harmony and beauty was hurt by the disharmony of the world in its innermost heart. Therefore he tried to heal wherever it seemed possible to him. Often the body, but mostly the mind.

Without exception, Krishnamurti was able to see both the weaknesses of people as well as their unawakened divine self. In this chapter I illustrate how far his mystic experiences outshined the abilities of the normal person. Krishnamurti was certainly not—or at least not any more—a human like everybody else; which was what many of his followers wanted him to be, as the affair centered on the *Notebook* demonstrated. He had been on his way into the "pathless land" for quite some time by then; and he had come closer to his destination, had been touched by its light. When Krishnamurti spoke of the "center of creation" or about "that which is," he spoke of the other shores of life, he spoke as a mystic ferry-man, moving across the river that divides time from eternity.

Healing

Krishnamurti did not want to be a healer—but he was one. He said in public: "I am concerned with the healing of the heart and the mind, not with the body."[338] In private, however, he laid hands on his friends repeatedly—as well as on strangers—to exercise the healing powers which even he was apparently unable to explain. "I do not know what that power is. I do not know how it works."[339] Krishnamurti had these healing powers from childhood. His mother had pointed out to him that he had "healing hands." Susunaga Weeraperuma reports conversations with Krishnamurti which show that he often used his powers but was not always successful. Apparently there were cases for which his healing powers did not work or where he was not permitted to help—for karmic reasons?

It is impossible to estimate the number of cases in which Krishnamurti was able to use his healing powers successfully. The documented cases only include those reported from the environment of the authors of the respective books, but what fraction of his huge sphere of activity were they able to record? Nearly every author of a book on Krishnamurti writes about exceptional healing experiences. Mary Lutyens writes about Radha Burnier's niece who was threatened by blindness, as was her brother, and for both, Krishnamurti was able to prevent it.[340] Weeraperuma writes about a female patient who was healed of deafness.[341] Rodney Field describes the healing session for his sick eyes, a session which was quite moving for him.[342] Pupul Jayakar reports that in Bombay Nandini Metha secretly brought ill children to Krishnamurti. Among them was an older boy who the doctors had said would never be able to see normally again because of a damaged optic nerve. Krishnamurti laid his hands on him and during the following years the condition of the boy improved so much that he was able to undertake university studies and was eventually awarded a Ph.D. from the University of California at Berkeley.[343] From the perspective of a patient, Vimala Thakar provides a moving description of a healing session when she writes: "He washed his hands. He walked gently. He stood behind my chair. He laid his right palm on my head; and his left palm over my left ear.

"I was alert. I saw that a very strong and forceful current of vibrations passed through the head and went through the whole body. The body became wonderfully relaxed. My eyes closed of their own accord. Krishnaji removed his hands. I tried to open my eyes. I could not focus them properly. It was like coming from a land of peace and light."[344]

Sometimes a healing session took only one or two minutes, as happened with Rohit Mehta who's spine Krishnamurti touched briefly, but those few minutes were enough to cure a paraplegic. Within a week Mehta was able to sit and he was walking after two months, to the astonishment of his doctors.[345]

While Krishnamurti himself preferredto reject his healing powers, he strongly encouraged others to accept similar talents and to use them for the sake of humanity. As an example, he reminded Nandini Mehta in vivid words: "You know about the baby they have been bringing to me. The doctor had said its brain had not formed. It could not see, could not smile, could not recognize, and I have been touching it. Something is functioning very strongly in me.

"I feel a burning in my hand and the baby has begun to smile, to recognize people. You can do it. All you have to do is to pick it up. The thing that is operating in me will work with you as well, pick it up. It is no use saying you don't know how. I say to you, pick it up."[346] For Krishnamurti, the healing act was a holy act, an act of mystic devotion to a higher power. Perhaps the question of whether he really did not know what was happening during the healing or whether he just did not want to speak about it will never be answered. However, there is no doubt that Krishnamurti himself was an example of the wonderful divine healing power which is effective everywhere where there is love.

Reincarnation

If you really believed in reincarnation,
your way of thinking, your lack of compassion,
and your indifference towards others would vanish,
because you have to pay for it in your next life,
you have to suffer.

In Part I, I touched upon Krishnamurti's view of the idea of reincarnation and referred to his disapproving statements, especially about the idea of evolution. Now, I give more space to his critical thoughts and the positive attitude he manifested in earlier times is compared with his later statements.

In 1928, Krishnamurti defined reincarnation as "a series of opportunities for the spiritual realization of pure being."[347] At the same time, he laid great stress on experiencing the living reality of reincarnation and not taking it as a mere theory. "It is a fact for me because I know it."[348] During the same talk at the Ommen camp in 1930, he gave a remarkable definition of karma. "Karma for me is the creation of a barrier between yourself and your ultimate growth. It is an

156

unconscious principle in life, not the private volition of any God. Please understand that. Your karma is what you make of it. It is beyond all control except by yourself. What you do bears a result which either makes for the destruction of barriers and hence freedom, or for their creation. It is you, therefore, who are responsible. The principle itself is mechanical and unconscious. It has nothing to do with private divine vengeance."[349] Krishnamurti never took a clear position against the truth of the teachings of reincarnation and karma, even though it sometimes sounded as if he did (see Notes 222 and 223). One must always analyze his critical statements very carefully so as not to interpret them incorrectly. For example, his statement during a talk at the Claremont College in California: "You know, the whole of Asia is conditioned to accept the theory of reincarnation; they discuss it a great deal and write about it, and they have invested their entire lives in the hope and fulfillment of their *next* life, but they overlook one very important point. If you are going to be born again, surely it is very important to live rightly in this life, so it matters tremendously what you do *now,* what you think, how you behave, how you talk and how your thought functions because according to your actions in this life your next life will be determined; there may be retribution. However they seem to forget all this and instead talk endlessly about the beauty of reincarnation, the justice of it and all that trivial nonsense."[350] Krishnamurti does not believe that the idea of reincarnation is nonsense but he believes that the perversion of its essence certainly is. It is important to act consciously and correctly in the present, knowing about future effects, and not trusting that 'in the next life everything will be better.' In addition, this criticism should be viewed in light of the radicalism of a true mystic who refuses to negotiate or even bargain with God. It is not to gain a better reincarnation that one should act rightly. Rather, the good deed is a demand of true insight. "There is no 'I shall be born again next life.' That is an idea to which you're attached. It gives you great comfort, but if you believe in reincarnation, then you must act rightly now, because next life you are going to pay for it or be rewarded. It's a very comforting idea, but it is meaningless. Because, if you act rightly now, righteousness has no reward. Righteousness is righteousness, not what you are going to get out of it. That is a merchandising attitude, a mechanical attitude."[351] This quote from one of his last talks does not present a 'new' Krishnamurti who, so to say, puts down his old ideas, but stands for the continuity of a clear insight which Krishnamurti had already expressed in 1931. "For me reincarnation is a fact and not a belief; but I do not want you to believe in reincarnation. On the contrary reject it; put it out of your mind; and remember only that as you are the product of the past, so you can control the future. You are the master of yourself and in your own hand lies eternity."[352]

His conflicts with the Theosophical Society had shown Krishnamurti, in a quite dramatic way, how the misunderstanding of esoteric knowledge could prevent any form of spiritual growth. Perhaps this is the key to several contradictory statements, especially regarding the question of a reincarnating individual. Insight into the truth of reincarnation should lead to focussed, correct action right now and not to comfortable 'what I cannot do today, I will do tomorrow.' The 'tomorrow' can only be a product of the 'today.' The transformation has to take place in the 'Now,' in the 'ewige Nu,' as Meister Eckhart expressed it.

Higher Worlds

Along with his healing power, Krishnamurti was extraordinarily clairvoyant even as a child. "When I was a boy...I used to see devas, angels and so on."[353] He kept this ability his whole life, though it vanished for a certain time after puberty and in the early twenties. In a letter to C. W. Leadbeater, Krishnamurti states that his clairvoyance returned to him on August 10, 1922. "I have become since that date much more sensitive and slightly clairvoyant as I saw you with the President, the other night while I was sitting in the moonlight. Such a thing has not happened to me for over seven years."[354] It seems doubtful whether Mary Lutyens' assumption is correct that Krishnamurti had already begun to suppress his higher perceptive faculties in the late twenties.[355] He certainly did not use them as a means for pure curiosity, but such a comment is unnecessary in any case considering Krishnamurti's character. He still possessed a remarkable clairvoyance, as was demonstrated by the description on an event passed on to us by Rodney Field. In the early seventies, he was on a walk with Krishnamurti on the beach at Malibu and mentioned casually: "'I suppose if one could see clairvoyantly out there the place wouldn't appear so empty,' I said.

"'People, sea elementals...'

"He interrupted. 'The place is full of them. I pay no attention to them.'

"'Do you see them every time you come out here?'

"'Only when I want to.'

"Since the subject had been broached, I took this opportunity to ask him about Invisible Helpers. 'Do such people really exist?'

"'Why not?' he said. 'Any decent person in this world will help another when in need. Why not on the other side? What's so special about it?'"[356] There are several references to similar experiences with Krishnamurti's clairvoyance. For example, during a personal talk Krishnamurti encouraged a Swedish healer to continue with her work, especially because "two angels were at her side"—a story I was told personally in Saanen. Krishnamurti spoke about this topic with a small circle of friends and acquaintances, often hidden behind a humorous anecdote. Pupul Jayakar described one such anecdote: "The atmosphere was pulsating, strong, alive. At one point he said, 'They found me two angels—I have gathered many more through the years.' He was laughing; there was a great laughter, and in between he kept saying, 'I am very serious.' He had not laughed like this in years. 'Now I find that I can do without some of them.' He turned to Radha and said, 'Can I give you two?' He was laughing, joyous, but deeply serious, suggesting something."[357]

In both his private and his public life, he dealt with the beings of darkness as well. In a small temple in Tetu one such occurrence took place, as described by Mary Lutyens. "On the way back, K told Mary that he had felt 'something following' him. He had 'done something' and said to it, 'That's enough,' and it had stopped immediately. A few days later when they walked again in Tetu, K said that he 'did something at the temple and told it to stay in its place.'"[358] In special cases, Krishnamurti seemed to have helped in guiding the deceased into the other world. This probably occurred in a special form at the death of Indira Gandhi. During those hours after the murder of the Indian Prime Minister, he sat meditating in silence. "At four in the afternoon he had felt Indira's presence and had commented on the need for silence within the mind to enable her to be at peace. I could see that he was deeply moved. Late the next night he was to say, 'Don't hold memories of Indira in your mind, that holds her to the earth. Let her go.' His hand made a gesture towards space and eternity."[359] An event that reminds one of the death of Nitya whom he had also seen clairvoyantly after his passing into the other world.

Krishnamurti's clairvoyance was important in connection with his healing power as well. Susunaga Weeraperuma reports the remarkable healing of an Englishman who was ill with tuberculosis and whose illness Krishnamurti had discovered immediately after they met. The report also gives an impressive description of another of Krishnamurti's healing sessions: "One afternoon I (the ill Englishman, P.M.) visited Krishnamurti without making a prior appointment. You see, I wanted to get his advice about whether to have an operation. He was walking out of the gates. He said: 'Please excuse me. I've had a busy day and I'm too tired to meet you. I'm going for a stroll. You may accompany me if you wish.' I agreed. So we walked together for a long time through meadows and fields and he hardly spoke. When we were standing on a bare stretch of land, Krishnamurti said: 'The moment I saw you I recognized your illness. My brother had the same trouble.' He then asked me not to feel any fear: 'Don't be scared.' The next thing that happened was that his fingers started running over my vertebral column. He rubbed my spine with his hands. I felt an upsurge of heat that started moving in the direction of my head. I felt a burning sensation in the upper part of the body. There was an uneasy heaviness and I was about to collapse. He held me firmly and helped me to walk back to his house. A few weeks later I felt stronger in body and my health definitely improved. Tests were carried out and the doctors pronounced that the diseased lung was no longer diseased. There was no need for an operation."[360] It seems likely to me that Krishnamurti not only used his clairvoyance for the diagnosis but also for the healing itself. Through his clear vision, he was able to direct the healing force well aimed.

As is true for many other fields, Krishnamurti's criticism of clairvoyance is not directed to the phenomenon as such, but to its perversion. Similar to his distortion of the Masters, meditation, spiritual healing or the worship of the holy, clairvoyance, too, served as a basis for several spiritual faux pas': "Always be skeptical of persons who claim to have clairvoyance. It is not that clairvoyance does not exist. It certainly exists. But doesn't it feed your vanity to believe that you have gifts lacking in others?"[361] In his warning, Krishnamurti is acting according to old Indian tradition, which states that the appearance of spiritual powers is regarded as a danger and as a level stretch on the path which must be overcome. For example, somebody who did not take clairvoyance as a kind of natural reality, similar to the normal senses, was in danger of losing the true goal of the spiritual path. "You may be clairvoyant or clairaudiant; but if there is not in you that spirit of all-inclusive thought, of love, that exquisite poise of these two, then of what value is your ability to see something invisible? It is irrelevant to your true purpose."[362] Again, Krishnamurti's radicalism becomes clear. No spiritual ability or power was important in itself. Only if it was used as a tool for the divine love and helped one to approach the absolute mind did Krishnamurti accept its value.

162

Transformation

Mystical experiences determined Krishnamurti's entire life and cannot be separated from his teachings. It is a radical and distorting contraction to reduce Krishnamurti's being to the factual message of his talks. The transformations of consciousness, the clear experience of higher worlds characterizes the spiritual dimension of Krishnamurti in a critical way. He was confronted with out-of-body experiences at an early age, many of which are documented in his personal notes. In one of his letters from 1922 he writes: "Then I could feel the vibrations of the Lord Buddha; I beheld Lord Maitreya and Master K. H. I was so happy, calm and at peace. I could still see my body and I was hovering near it. There was such profound calmness both in the air and within myself, the calmness of the bottom of a deep unfathomable lake. Like the lake, I felt my physical body, with its mind and emotions, could be ruffled on the surface but nothing, nay nothing, could disturb the calmness of my soul."[363] In one of the conversations from the Ommen camp in 1926, he refers to an experiment he tried with himself in Ooctacamund, India. "I remember when I was at Ooty, in the Nilgiris in India, I was experimenting with myself, not very successfully at first, trying to discover how I could detach myself and see the body as it is. I had been experimenting with it for two or three days, it may have been a week; and I found that for a certain length of time I could quite easily be away from the body and look at it. I was standing beside my bed, and there was the body on the bed— a most extraordinary feeling. And from that day there has been a distinct sense of detachment, of division between the ruler and the ruled, so that the body, though it has its cravings, its desires to wander forth and to live and enjoy separately for itself, does not in any way interfere with the true self."[364] These experiences were preliminary stages of his own spiritual path, which was to guide him later in higher realms of realization; but even as intermediate stages they cannot be neglected. Interestingly, these phases of transformation were frequently connected to a stay in India. Also, Krishnamurti seemed to have referred more often to esoteric teachings when he was in India than in Europe. For example, when he was doing Yoga with the daughter and nephew of Pupul Jayakar: "He showed them how to walk, how to stand, how to see from the back of the head. This was to let seeing flow backwards and to see from depth. He took them for long walks, observing, listening, and teaching them to see and listen."[365] Even though he was quite cosmopolitan and made strong claims to be so, it is probably true that in a hidden corner of his heart he was convinced that India, the country of the great Rishis, still held a door to the Holy, the Divine. This sometimes led to inconsistencies. On the one hand, he disqualified the use of mantras in meditation as nonsense and dulling self-hypnosis, and yet on the other hand, he noted in his *Journal*: "The sound of Sanskrit chants seems to have a strange effect. In a temple, about fifty priests were chanting in Sanskrit and the very walls seemed to be vibrating."[366] But perhaps, as Mary Lutyens points out, this inconsistency illustrates his humanity and shows that Krishnamurti was not a perfect being.

When Krishnamurti spoke about esoteric questions, his extremely high standard and his blunt criticism of self-made gurus became apparent. Krishnamurti abhorred the highly intellectual prattle spoken by those who were not working on their own imperfections. "The people who speak of the awakening of Kundalini, I question. They have not worked at the other, but say they have awakened Kundalini. Therefore, I question their ability, their truth. I am not antagonistic, but I am questioning it. A man who eats meat, wants publicity, wants this and that and says his Kundalini is awakened, I say it is nonsense. There must be a cleansing of this house all the time.... There is an energy which is renewing itself all the time, which is not mechanistic, which has no cause, which has no beginning and therefore no ending. It is an eternal movement. I say there is. What value has it to the listener? I say 'yes' and you listen to me. I say to myself what value has that to you? Will you go off into that and not clear up the house?"[367]

Krishnamurti's reserve regarding certain transformational processes can be explained in part by his conviction that experiences could not be explained with old patterns or models, nor in traditional words. The experience could only be shared and understood via a direct, personal experience, such as, for example, the transformation of one's cell structure. "Memory is stored in the brain cells. When the mind is fully transformed the very brain cells experience a mutation. It is a fundamental change which cannot be explained in scientific terms. Unless you have personally experienced this mutation you will not know what I am talking about."[368] The question remains whether Krishnamurti regarded transformational processes, like the ones he experienced himself, as a normal stage on the path of spiritual growth, or whether each seeker had to gain his or her own different experiences. However, if one compares his experiences with those known to esoteric tradition, one recognizes that these are not such unusual phenomena.

Mysticism of Nature

I saw Him fill the sky and the blade of grass.
I saw Him in the heights of the trees. I beheld Him
in the pebble, everywhere, and I saw Him in myself!
Therefore my temple was filled
and my Holy of Holiest was completed.
I was Him, He was I, and this was my Truth.

With the exception of St. Francis of Assisi, Krishnamurti lived closer to nature than almost any other great mystic of history. He sensed the infinitely deep consciousness of the rocks with their memories of eons; he met the trees with deep respect and, for example, on walks during the Saanen meetings, before he entered the forest, he would ask: "May we enter?" Animals sensed his gentle nature and approached him without shyness. A Langur ape once came to him, looked at him for some time and then gave him his strong but soft hand, despite its calluses, like one friend to the other. In Rishi Valley, he talked to a Hoopoe bird as he would to an old friend. No being was ever too insignificant for him;[369] because all life in nature was part of his own life and his being was part of his own inner space (Welteninnenraum).

In Krishnamurti's view, the problem of people in the industrial age was that they had lost their reverence for nature and the respect for its mysteries. However, only if those qualities could be found again would nature lift the veil of invisibility before its creatures. "A plant wrongly approached, with greed or desire, vanishes and cannot be found. Plants and herbs have to be talked to. Their permission must be taken before touching them, they have to be addressed with humility—'Do you permit me to touch you, would you like me to wait?' They give light and fragrance to those who commune with them."[370] The key to the door of the mysterious kingdoms of nature could be found in the hearts of each individual and one of the keys is beauty. His notes in his journals, with some of its deep wordings, give a glimpse on Krishnamurti's access to nature and reveal his admiration for its beauty. For example, in one of his talks to himself about two lilies: "The two lilies were the delight of the whole garden, even the large trees looked down upon them without shadow; they were delicate, soft and quiet in their pond. When you looked at them, all reaction ceased, your thoughts and feelings faded away and only they remained, in their beauty and their quietness; they were intense, like every living thing is, except man who is so everlastingly occupied with himself. As you watched these two, the world was changed, not into some better social order, with less tyranny and more freedom or poverty eliminated, but there was no pain, no sorrow, the coming and going of anxiety and there was no toil of boredom; it was changed because those two were there, blue with golden hearts. It was the miracle of beauty."[371]

But Krishnamurti's special love was for the trees. The secluded weeks he spent in the Giant Forest of Sequoia National Park, California, rank among the most beautiful of his life. In the following paragraphs, I quote two of Krishnamurti's statements about trees. The first quote is taken from a talk he gave in Saanen, the second one is a note from his *Journal* dated October 20, 1973. In my view, there is no better way to distinguish between what I believe to be the 'official' and the 'true' Krishnamurti. It is not difficult to differentiate which is which. Krishnamurti said during his talk: "One may commune with a tree, for example, or with a mountain, or a river. I do not know if you have ever sat beneath a tree and really tried to commune with it. It is not sentimentality, it is not emotionalism—you are directly in contact with the tree. There is an extraordinary intimacy of relationship. In such communion, there must be silence, there must be a deep sense of quietness; your heart itself almost comes to a stop. There is no interpretation, there is no communication, no sharing. The tree is not you, nor are you identified with the tree; there is only this sense of intimacy in a great depth of silence."[372]

His note in his *Journal* refers to the hours he spent in meditative silence beneath one of those gigantic redwood trees. For one who has not experienced the majesty of those exalted beings, it may be difficult to understand what Krishnamurti wants to express in his exposition. But a hint of this magic will touch them nevertheless. "The noisy tourists had not come yet and you could be alone with its great silent one; it soared up to the heavens as you sat under it, vast and timeless. Its very years gave it the dignity of silence and the aloofness of great age. It was as silent as your mind was, as still as your heart, and living without the burden of time. You were aware of compassion that time had never touched and of innocence that had never known hurt and sorrow. You sat there and time passed you by and it would never come back. There was immortality, for death had never been. Nothing existed except that immense tree, the clouds and the earth. You went to that tree and sat down with it and every day for many days it was a benediction of which you were only aware when you wandered away. You could never come back to it asking for more; there was never more, the more was in the valley far below. Because it was not a man-made shrine, there was unfathomable sacredness which would never again leave you, for it was not yours."[373]

168

Unio Mystica

*One night I woke feeling the whole universe converge
into me. An entering of everything and a traveling
deeper and deeper into a depth without end.*

From the "uniting with the Beloved," as the young
Krishnamurti called it, to the touching of "the nameless
source, the absolute silence," thus named by him during his
last sentences he spoke in public—the experience of 'unio'
(unity) was the core of his life. His thoughts revolved around
this inexpressible mystery repeatedly, a mystery that he always tried to grasp with words. An effort that was doomed
to failure, as it had been for all other mystics before him.
He who had no ears to hear, did not hear anything; and she
who had no eyes did not see anything.

In 1931, Krishnamurti talked in Ommen about one of his
realizations which had occurred five years earlier. "I realized in 1926 something that is ultimate, fundamental, that
has no direction. Please understand, this is not progressive,
but something that is absolute though not a finality; it is a
constant renewal, being Life itself; it is a timeless becoming and cannot be measured with words."[374] Other experiences had preceded this major experience of unity, including the one he described in his letter from August 1922 and
from which I have already quoted. "On the first day while I
was in that state and more conscious of the things around
me, I had the first most extraordinary experience. There was
a man mending the road; that man was myself; the pickax
he held was myself; the very stone which he was breaking
up was a part of me; the tender blade of grass was my very
being, and the tree beside the man was myself. I almost

169

could feel and think like the road mender, and I could feel the wind passing through the tree, and the little ant on the blade of grass I could feel. The birds, the dust, and the very noise were a part of me. Just then there was a car passing by at some distance; I was the driver, the engine, and the tires; as the car went further away from me, I was going away from myself. I was in everything, or rather everything was in me, inanimate and animate, the mountain, the worm, and all breathing things."[375]

In 1961, nearly forty years later, the dynamic of that mystical process of experience is still unbroken. The pages of his *Notebook* from July 20, 1961, contain one of most moving testimonies of Krishnamurti's experiences and comprise one of the great, timeless documents of the mystical experience of unity. "The room became full with that benediction. Now what followed is almost impossible to put down in words; words are such dead things, with definite set meaning and what took place was beyond all words and description. It was the center of all creation; it was a purifying seriousness that cleansed the brain of every thought and feeling; its seriousness was as lightning which destroys and burns up; the profundity of it was not measurable, it was there immovable, impenetrable, a solidity that was as light as the heavens. It was in the eyes, in the breath. It was in the eyes and the eyes could see. The eyes that saw, that looked were wholly different from the eyes of the organ and yet they were the same eyes. There was only seeing, the eyes that saw beyond timespace. There was impenetrable dignity and a peace that was the essence of all movement, action."[376]

What distinguishes Krishnamurti from the mystic who is happy in his self-immersion, is his unceasing readiness to let his light shine *in the world* and his conviction about the social importance of mystical transformation. The mystic does not only transform *his* lower self, but in his metamorphosis the whole of humanity is changed. "As we pointed out, if a few really understand what we have been telling about for the last fifty years, and are really deeply involved and have brought about the end of fear, sorrow and so on, then that will affect the whole of the consciousness of mankind."[377]

I have no doubt that Krishnamurti was one of the few 'Great in Spirit' who was touched by the light of God. His boundless love and his deep humility opened the door through which the spirit could enter. In contrast to the traditional Advaita, that of a Ramana Maharishi for example, Krishnamurti did not believe that his experience was the end of all possible experiences. Rather, the depth of his vision made him touch—as did Sri Aurobindo at the same time— the immensity of the absolute and see, with all potential divinity, the limitation of human knowledge. He expressed this quite movingly during a very personal conversation with Susunaga Weeraperuma. He remembers: "Believe me, I only see a fragment of the Infinite."[378] With this statement, Krishnamurti's revolutionary approach continues on the lowest level. The 'unio mystica,' until then regarded as the final experience, gains a new dynamic through his insight. It is to be understood no longer as the end but as the beginning, as Krishnamurti had already indicated in his theosophical period when he characterized illumination not as destruction but as a new beginning. The experience of the Divine has no ending, is always new, filled with indescribable beauty and glory. IT will always be a mystery. "It's not possible to be one with it; it is not possible to be one with a swiftly flowing river. You can never be one with that which has no form, no measure, no quality. It is; that is all."[379]

171

Bibliography

I. Works by Krishnamurti

Action, Krishnamurti Foundation of America: Ojai, 1990.

A Dialogue With Oneself, Krishnamurti Foundation of America: Ojai, 1977.

A Flame of Learning, Mirananda: Den Haag, 1993.

At the Feet of the Master (Alcyone), The Theosophical Publishing House: Wheaton, 1989.

By What Authority, Star Publishing Trust: Ommen, 1928.

Choiceless Awareness, Krishnamurti Foundation of America: Ojai, 1991.

Collected Works, Vol. 1-17, Kendall/ Hunt Publications: New York, 1980.

Conversations, Krishnamurti Foundation of America: Ojai, 1970.

Commentaries on Living, Vol. 1-3, The Theosophical Publishing House: Wheaton, 1992.

Early Talks, Vol. 1-7, Chetana: Bombay, 1972.

Early Writings, Vol. 1-7, Chetana: Bombay, 1969.

Education and the Significance of Life, Harper & Row: San Francisco, 1953.

Exploration into Insight, V. Gollancz: London, 1979.

Freedom From the Self, Krishnamurti Foundation India: Madras, 1991.

Freedom from the Known, Harper & Row: San Francisco, 1969.

Individual and Society: The Bondage of Conditioning, Krishnamurti Foundation of America: Ojai, 1991.

Inward Flowering, Krishnamurti Foundation of America: Ojai, 1977.

Krishnamurti at Los Alamos, Krishnamurti Foundation of America: Ojai, 1984.

Krishnamurti at Rajghat, Krishnamurti Foundation India: Madras, 1993.

Krishnamurti on Education, Krishnamurti Foundation India: Madras, 1974.

Krishnamurti on Freedom, Harper San Francisco: San Francisco, 1991.

Krishnamurti on God, Harper San Francisco: San Francisco, 1992.

Krishnamurti on Living and Dying, Harper San Francisco: San Francisco, 1992.

Krishnamurti on Nature and the Environment, Harper San Francisco: San Francisco, 1991.

Krishnamurti on Relationship, Harper San Francisco: San Francisco, 1992.

Krishnamurti on Right Livelihood, Harper San Francisco: San Francisco, 1992.

Krishnamurti Talks, Verbatim Reports, Vol. 1-9, Krishnamurti Foundation India: Madras, 1934.

Krishnamurti to Himself, Harper San Francisco: San Francisco, 1993.

Krishnamurti's Journal, Harper & Row: San Francisco, 1982.

Krishnamurti's Notebook, Harper San Francisco: San Francisco, 1976.

Last Talks at Saanen 1985, Harper & Row: San Francisco, 1985.

Later Talks, Vol. 1-7, Chetana: Bombay, 1974.

Letters to the Schools, Vol. 1, Mirananda: Den Haag, 1981.

Letters to the Schools, Vol. 2, Mirananda: Wassenaar, 1985.

174

Meditations, Krishnamurti Foundation India: Madras, 1979. (pocket book edition: Shambhala: Berkeley, 1990).

Meeting Life, Harper San Francisco: San Francisco, 1991.

Mind Without Measure, Krishnamurti Foundation India: Madras, 1984.

On Love, Krishnamurti Foundation Trust: London, 1980.

Questions and Answers, Krishnamurti Foundation Trust: London, 1982.

Reden am Feuer, Diederichs: Jena, 1929.

Social Responsibility, Krishnamurti Foundation of America: Ojai, 1992.

Special Memorial Bulletin # 53, Krishnamurti Foundation of America: Ojai, 1986.

Sri Lanka Talks 1980, Krishnamurti Foundation India: Madras, 1980.

Talks and Dialogues Saanen 1967, Avon Books: New York, 1967.

Talks and Dialogues Saanen 1968, Krishnamurti Foundation Trust: London, 1970.

Talks with American Students, Shambhala: Berkeley, 1968.

The Awakening of Intelligence, Harper & Row: San Francisco, 1973.

The Ending of Time, Harper & Row: San Francisco, 1985.

The First and Last Freedom, Harper & Row: San Francisco, 1954.

The Flame of Attention, Harper & Row: San Francisco, 1983.

The Flight of the Eagle, Harper & Row: New York, 1973.

The Future is Now, Harper & Row: San Francisco, 1989.

The Future of Humanity, Mirananda: Den Haag, 1986.

The Impossible Question, Arkana: London, 1991.

The Mirror of Relationship: Love, Sex, and Chastity, Krishnamurti Foundation of America: Ojai, 1992.

The Network of Thought, Harper & Row: San Francisco, 1982.
The Only Revolution, V. Gollancz: London, 1970.
The Path, Star Publ. Trust: Ommen, 1930.
The Search, Star Publ. Trust: New York, 1927.
The Second Penguin Krishnamurti Reader, Penguin Books: London, 1970.
The Way of Intelligence, Krishnamurti Foundation India: Madras, 1985.
The Wholeness of Life, Harper & Row: San Francisco, 1978.
Things of the Mind, Motilal Banarsidass: Delhi, 1985.
Think on these Things, Harper & Row: San Francisco, 1964.
Towards Discipleship, The Theosophical Publishing House: Adyar, 1926.
Tradition and Revolution, Krishnamurti Foundation India: Madras, 1972.
Washington D.C. Talks 1985, Mirananda: Den Haag, 1988.
World of Peace / Welt des Friedens, Jadrny Verlag: Munich, 1985.
You are the World, Harper & Row: New York, 1972.

Collections

I. v. Massenbach, *Ausgewählte Texte*, Goldmann: Munich, 1988.
S. Weeraperuma, *A Bibliography of the Life and Teachings of J.K.*, E. J. Drill: Leiden, 1984.
S. Weeraperuma, *A Supplement to a Bibliography of the Life and Teachings of J.K.*, Chetana: Bombay, 1982.
S. Weeraperuma, *Sayings of Krishnamurti*, Chetana: Bombay, 1986.

II. Secondary Literature

Anrias, David, *Adepts of the Five Elements*, E. P. Dutton: New York, 1934.

Anrias, David, *Through the Eyes of the Masters*, Routledge & Kegan: London, 1976.

Baker, Gladys, *Krishnamurti-Who Is He*, The Birmingham New-Age Herald, April 4, 1929.

Balfour-Clarke, Russel, *The Boyhood of J. Krishnamurti*, Chetana: Bombay, 1977.

Besant, Annie, *World Teacher*, Herald of the Star, 1/1913, p. 5.

Besant, Annie, *Die Arbeit des Weltlehrers*, Talk in Vienna Sept. 2, 1927, unpublished.

Burnier, Radha, *Krishnaji's Challenge*, The American Theosophist, Vol. 75/10, p. 344.

Chandmal, Asit, *One Thousand Moons*, Abrams: New York, 1985.

Coleman, John E., *The Quiet Mind*, Rider: London, 1971.

Desikachar, T. K. V., *Krishnaji--The Student and the Teacher*, Krishnamacharya Yoga Mandiram: Madras (no year).

Dhopeshwarkar, A. D., *K. and Mind in Revolution*, Chetana: Bombay, 1976.

Dhopeshwarkar, A. D., *Meditation a la K.*, Chetana: Bombay, 1978.

Dhopeshwarkar, A. D., *K. and the Experience of the Silent Mind*, Chetana: Bombay, 1981.

Dhopeshwarkar, A. D., *The Yoga of J. K.*, Chetana: Bombay, 1981.

Dhopeshwarkar, A. D., *K. and the Texture of Reality*, Chetana: Bombay, 1982.

Field, Sidney, *K.—The Reluctant Messiah*, Paragon: New York, 1989.

Fouere, Rene, *K.: The Man and His Teaching*, Chetana: Bombay, 1981.

Grohe, Friedrich, *The Beauty of the Mountains: Memories of Krishnamurti*, Krishnamurti Foundation Trust: Bramdean, 1991.

Heber, Lilly, *Krishnamurti*, Allan & Unwin: London, 1931.

Heider, Norbert, *Die pädagogisch-psychologische Konzeption der Krishnamurti-Schulen*, Mag.-Arbeit, Universität Regensburg: Regensburg, 1992.

Hodson, Geoffrey, Herald of the Star, 10/1924, p. 422.

Hodson, Geoffrey, *Camp Fire Gleams*, Hearald of the Star 10/1927, p. 403.

Hodson, Geoffrey, *Thus have I Heard*, The Theosophical Publishing House: Adyar, 1947.

Hodson, Geoffrey, *K. and the Search for Light*, (no place, no year).

Hodson, Sandra, and Thiel, M. van, *C. W. Leadbeater—The Great Seer*, unpublished manuscript.

Holroyd, Stuart, *The Quest for the Quiet Mind*, Aquarian: Wellingborough, 1983.

Holroyd, Stuart, *The Man, the Mystery and the Message*, Element: Rockport, 1991.

Huchzermeyer, Wilfried, *Krishnamurti und der Taoismus*, Eigenverlag Huchzermeyer: Karlsruhe, 1991.

Jayakar, Pupul, *Krishnamurti—A Biography*, Harper & Row: San Francisco, 1986.

Landau, Rom, *God is My Adventure*, Nicholson & Watson: London, 1964.

Leadbeater, Charles W., *48 Lifes of Alcyone*, unpublished manuscript.

Leadbeater, Charles W., *A Momentous Incident*, Herald of the Star, 1/1912, p. 33.

Leadbeater, Charles W., and Besant, Annie, *Talks on the Path of Occultism*, Vol.I: *At the Feet of the Master*, The Theosophical Publishing House: Adyar, 1926.

Lutyens, Emily, *Candles in the Sun*, Rupert Hart-Davis: London, 1957.

Lutyens, Mary, *Krishnamurti—Years of Awakening*, Avon Books: New York, 1983.

Lutyens, Mary, *Krishnamurti—The Years of Fulfillment*, Avon Books: New York, 1983.

Lutyens, Mary, *Krishnamurti—The Open Door*, Avon Books: New York, 1988.

Lutyens, Mary, *Krishnamurti—His Life and Death*, Avon Books: New York, 1991.

Mehta, Rohit, *J.K. and the Nameless Experience*, Motilal Banarsidass Publishers: Bombay, 1979.

Mehta, Rohit, *The Intuitive Philosophy*, Motilal Banarsidass Publishers: Bombay, 1988.

Methorst-Kuiper, A. J. G., *Krishnamurti*, 2nd Edition, Chetana: Bombay, 1976.

Miners, Scott (ed.), *A Spiritual Approach to Male/Female Relations*, The Theosophical Publishing House: Wheaton, 1984, p. 32.

Nahal, C. L., *A Conversation with J. K.*, Arya Bode Depot: New Delhi, 1965.

Nearing, Helen, *Loving and Leaving the Good Life*, Chelsea Greeen Publishing: Post Mill, 1992.

Nethercot, Arthur H., *The Last Four Lives of Annie Besant*, The University of Chicago Press: Chicago, 1963.

Niel, Andre, *K. the Man in Revolt*, Chetana: Bombay, 1982.

Peacocke, C. L., *An Historical Meeting*, Herald of the Star 2/1912, p. 40.

Prasad, N. Lakshmi, *Real Change is Revolutionary*, The Quest 4/1990, p. 75.

Rajneesh, Osho, *K.—Gescheiterte Verkündung*, Connection 6/1989.

Ransom, Josephine, *A Short History of the Theosophical Society*, The Theosophical Publishing House: Adyar, 1938.

Ravindra, Ravi, *The Mill and the Mill Pond*, Krishnamurti Foundation of America: Ojai, (no year).

Robertson, John Kirk, *Aquarian Occultist*, unpublished biography on Hodson.

Ryzek, Marianne, *Über K.*, Edition Geflechte: Eurasburg, 1985.

Scott, Cyril, *The Initiate*, Samuel Weiser: York Beach, 1971.

Scott, Cyril, *The Initiate in the Dark Cycle*, Samuel Weiser: York Beach, 1991.

Scott, Cyril, *The Initiate in the New World*, Samuel Weiser: York Beach, 1991.

Singh, Shashi, *K. Remembered*, The American Theosophist, 10/1987, p. 348.

Sloss, Radha Rajagopal, *Lives in the Shadow with J. K.*, Bloomsbury Publishing: London, 1991.

Smith, Ingram, *Truth is a Pathless Land*, The Theosophical Publishing House: Wheaton, 1989.

Suares, Carlo, *K. and the Unity of Man*, Chetana: Bombay, 1982.

Thakar, Vimala, *On an Eternal Voyage*, Vimala Thakar Foundation: Holland, 1974.

Tillet, Gregory, *The Elder Brother*, Routledge & Kegan Paul: London, 1982.

Torwesten, Hans, *Befreiung vom Antiguru*, Connection, 6/ 1989.

Vas, Luis S. R. (Ed.), *The Mind of J. K.*, Jaico Publishing House: Bombay, 1975.

Vitelleschi, C., *Ethik als Tat*, Diederichs: Jena, 1930.

Weber, Renee, *Dialogues with Scientists and Sages*, Arkana: London, 1990.

Weeraperuma, Susunaga, *Bliss of Reality*, Chetana: Bombay, 1984.

Weeraperuma, Susunaga, *Living and Dying*, Chetana: Bombay, 1987.

Weeraperuma, Susunaga, *That Pathless Land*, Chetana: Bombay, 1987.

Weeraperuma, Susunaga, *K. as I Knew Him*, Chetana: Bombay, 1988.

White, John (ed.), *What is Enlightenment*, Los Angeles, 1984.

Wodehouse, E. A., *A Conversation with K.*, International Star Bulletin, 3/1930, p. 19.

Notes

Preface

1. See P. Michel, *Die Botschafter des Lichtes* , Vol. 1-2, Aquamarin Verlag: Forstinning, Germany, 1983.
2. Pupul Jayakar, *Krishnamurti*, Harper & Row: San Francisco, 1986, p. 2.
3. *Last Talks at Saanen*, Harper & Row: San Francisco, 1986.
4. Krishnamurti often talked about himself in the third person.
5. Jayakar, p. 12.
6. Pupul Jayakar participated in an international conference, organized by Aquamarin Verlag in Germany. The proceedings are published in: Petra Michel (ed.), *Wissenschaftler und Weise—Die Konferenz*, Aquamarin Verlag: Grafing, Germany, 1991.
7. See J. Krishnamurti, *Krishnamurti To Himself*, Harper San Francisco: San Francisco, 1993.
8. Susunaga Weeraperuma, *J. Krishnamurti as I Knew Him*, Chetana: Bombay, India, 1988, p. 103.

Part 1—The Life

9. About Krishnamurti's childhood see: Mary Lutyens, *Krishnamurti: His Life and Death*, Avon Books: New York, 1991, p. 1, and Jayakar, p. 15.

10. Personal note from J. Cordes to Prof. Karl Schmid, Freyung, Germany. Letter from K. Schmid to me dated August 4,1980. About the aura theory, see: Russell Balfour-Clarke, *The Boyhood of J. Krishnamurti*, Chetana: Bombay, India 1977, p. 3.

11. See Emily Lutyens, *Candles in the Sun*, Rupert Hart-Davis: London, England 1957, p. 27.

12. Jayakar, p. 26; but also see Mary Lutyens, *Krishnamurti—The Open Door*, John Murray: London, England 1988, p. 6.

13. Surprisingly enough, Pupul Jayakar does not mention one critical word about this important 'reincarnation' of Krishnamurti.

14. See the strange biography on C. W. Leadbeater by G. Tillett: Gregory Tillett, *The Elder Brother*, Routledge & Kegan Paul: London, England 1982, p. 10, which is shaped by a peculiar love-hate relationship of the author.

15. Jayakar, p. 405. 'Pax' is Latin for 'peace.'

16. Mary Lutyens, *Krishnamurti: The Years of Awakening*, Avon Books: New York, 1991, p. xiii.

17. See Balfour-Clarke, p. 72.

18. Mary Lutyens, *Awakening*, p. 156.

19. Balfour-Clarke, p. 9; also: Lutyens, *Awakening*, p. 29.

20. See Jayakar, p. 19.

21. Ibid., p. 20.

22. Ibid., p. 27; see also: Lutyens, *Life and Death*, Chapter 1.

23. *Krishnamurti's Journal*, London 1982, p. 11. On page 27 of the *Journal* the loss of his memory of his early childhood is mentioned.—In contrast, A. H. Nethercot writes in his biography of A. Besant about a paper, written in Gujerati by Mrs. Mangal Das, which includes a detailed description of the childhood of

Krishnamurti and which he himself had given to Mrs. Das. See: Arthur H. Nethercot, *The Last Four Lives of Annie Besant*, Chicago 1963, p. 135.

24. Jayakar, p. 292.
25. Balfour-Clarke, p. 5. See also ibid., p. 14.
26. Mary Lutyens, *Life and Death*, p. 12.
27. Jayakar, p. 28.
28. According to Tillett, who believes that certain magical rituals could be the basis for the connection of Krishna, Christ and the World Teacher; loc. cit., p. 107.
29. Annie Besant, *Talk in Vienna*, September 2, 1927 (re-translated into English). Besant states her ideas about the World Teacher in detail in two articles in the Herald of the Star: *The Order of the Star in the East*, 3/ 1912, and *World-Teachers*, 1/1913.
30. See Mariijn Brandt, *Keine Religion ist höher als die Wahrheit*, in: *C. W. Leadbeater* (eds. Sandra Hodson & M. van Thiel), unpublished German translation by J. Fleischanderl, p. 13 (copy with the author).
31. Annie Besant and C.W. Leadbeater, *Talks on the Path of Occultism,* Vol. I: *At the Feet of the Master*, The Theosophical Publishing House: London, 1926, p. 3.
32. Read about these events: Ingram Smith, *Truth is a Pathless Land*, The Theosophical Publishing House: Wheaton, 1989, p. 20.
33. Balfour-Clarke, p. 25.
34. E. Lutyens, *Candles*, p. 110.
35. Mary Lutyens, *Awakening*, p. 30.
36. Emily Lutyens thinks that a *mediumistic* transmission by Krishnamurti is a possibility. *Candles*, p. 28.
37. Also about the powerful impression: B.-Clarke, p. 18.
38. Jayakar, p. 364.

39. See: E. Lutyens, *Candles*, p. 67; Mary Lutyens, *Awakening*, p. 117; Lilly Heber, *Krishnamurti*, Allan & Unwin: London, 1931, p. 51.

40. See Mary Lutyens, ibid., pp. 90, 100.

41. Ibid., p. 121.

42. Ibid., p. 118.

43. Ibid., p. 162.

44. *Herald of the Star*, 1/1912.

45. See E. Lutyens, p. 142.

46. Talk in Vienna, 1927, loc. cit., p. 12 (retranslated into English).

47. Unfortunately, G. Hodson did not agree to have this biography published, as explained in a letter written to me by his wife Sandra. Therefore, I can only refer to the unpublished manuscript, of which I received a photocopy from one of G. Hodson's pupils.

48. G. Hodson, *Thus Have I Heard*, The Theosophical Publishing House: Adyar, 1947, p. 107. See also *Camp Fire Gleams*, Herald of the Star. 10/1927, p. 403.

48a. G. Hodson, *Light of the Sanctuary*, Manila, 1988.

49. Manuscript by Robertson, p. 196.

50. Mary Lutyens, *Awakening*, p. 289.

51. Herald of the Star, 2/1912, p. 33.

52. C.L. Peacocke, *An Historical Meeting*, Herald of the Star, 2/1912, p. 40.

53. Mary Lutyens, *Life and Death*, p. 40. If one takes into account the many documents which have been published about the mystical transformation of Krishnamurti, commonly referred to as 'The Process,' it is unbelievable how Radha Sloss came to the strange conclusion that Krishnamurti only faked The Process to attract women (see Sloss, p. 58). This demonstrates her considerable lack of knowledge about mystic trans-

formations, if not a willing attempt to twist the facts. There are grounds for this assumption because Radha Sloss writes in conjunction with The Process: "This time he refused to have Rosalind near him and occasionally called instead for the absent Helen, but mostly he wanted no one" (Sloss, p. 67). It is legitimate to question Krishnamurti's mystic transformation, but R. Sloss' approach seems to totally miss the reality of these events.

54. A. J. G. Methorst-Kuiper, *Krishnamurti*, 2nd Edition, Chetana: Bombay 1976, p. 21.

55. Mary Lutyens, *Awakening*, p. 173. See also E. Lutyens, p. 144, where Krishnamurti regards himself as an empty vessel, similar to a 'crystal vase.'

56. Jayakar, p. 48. See also Krishnamurti, *Reden am Feuer*, Diederichs: Jena, 1929, p. 59; Krishnamurti, *The Path*, 3rd Edition, Star Publishing Trust: Ommen 1930, p. 65, there Krishnamurti writes about himself: "I am God."

57. *Talk in Vienna*, loc. cit., p. 12 (retranslated into English).

58. Mary Lutyens, *Life and Death*, p. 70.

59. *A Discussion at Eerde*, International Star Bulletin, 11/1928, p. 9.

60. Ibid., p. 11.

61. *Early Writings II*, p. 116.

62. Gladys Baker, *Krishnamurti—Who is He?*, The Birmingham New-Age-Herald, 1.4.1929.

63. Mary Lutyens, *Awakening*, p. 236.

64. See Sidney Field, *Krishnamurti—The Reluctant Messiah*, Paragon: New York 1989, p. 52.

65. Mary Lutyens, loc. cit., p. 246.

66. Jayakar, p. 67.

67. *Early Writings V*, p. 131; see also ibid., p. 157.
68. Krishnamurti, *Editorial Notes*, Herald of the Star 1/ 1926. This remark is left out in all publications—intentionally? The quotes of this evidence of Krishnamurti's feelings after the death of his brother often end before the earlier paragraph.
69. Therefore, at the congress in Vienna in 1923 an attentive observer was able to record 'how much Krishnamurti was annoyed by the fuss about his person.' Stated by Prof. Karl Schmid in a letter to me from September 24, 1981, in which he wrote about his recollections from those years.
70. Mary Lutyens, loc. cit., p. 262.
71. Ibid., p. 281.
72. *Last Talks at Saanen*, p. 73.
73. E. Lutyens, loc. cit., p. 172.
74. Mary Lutyens, loc. cit., p. 293.
75. *Early Writings*, Vol. I, p. 67; Similarly in June 1926: "For many lives, and for all this life, and especially during the last few months, I have struggled to be free— free of my friends, my books, my associations" (Emily Lutyens, p. 160).
76. *Early Writings III*, p. 23.
77. Geoffrey Hodson, *Krishnamurti and the Search for Light*, The Theosophical Publishing House: Adyar (no year), p. 33. The consternation about his harshness, felt especially by those Theosophists who accompanied him from the beginning, is exemplified in the words Leadbeater spoke to Rukmini Arundale just before he died: "Am I an exploiter?" (Sloss, p. 119)
78. Mary Lutyens, *Awakening*, p. 300.
79. Jayakar, p. 439.
80. Mary Lutyens, *Awakening*, p. 306.

81. Hodson, loc. cit., p. 51.

82. See ibid., p. 63.

83. Regarding Krishnamurti's earlier self-doubts: Jayakar, p. 96.

84. Comments about this issue: Carlo Suares, *Krishnamurti and the Unity of Man*, Chetana: Bombay 19826, p. 65.

85. Mary Lutyens, *Awakening*, p. 303.

86. Mary Lutyens, *Krishnamurti—The Years of Fulfillment*, Avon Books: New York, 1984, p. 23.

87. S. Weeraperuma, *Supplement to a Bibliography of the Life and Teachings of Jiddu Krishnamurti*, Chetana: Bombay, 1982, p. 110. In addition, see the remarkable comments made by Radha Burnier, the President of the Theosophical Society, who is also Trustee of the Krishnamurti Foundation--the circle is made again. She wrote in an article from 1987: "H.P. Blavatsky warned that most organizations like ours do not survive for more than one hundred years. Generally they become encrusted with dogma and degenerate into some kind of sectarianism. The members tend to rest upon the oars of their past achievements, giving little attention to discovery and action in the present. If the Theosophical Society has escaped such a fate, it is in large measure due to Krishnaji's questioning and criticism. This may not have pleased all members of the Theosophical Society, but nonetheless it helped to restore vitality to the pursuit of the fundamental aims of the society." *The American Theosophist*, Fall Special Issue/1987, p. 345.

88. See the entire debate between Hodson and Krishnamurti: *Krishnamurti and the Search for Light*, loc. cit., p. 10.

89. Ingram Smith, *Truth is a Pathless Land*, loc. cit., p. 19.

90. S. Field, *Krishnamurti*, loc. cit., p. 53.
91. Jayakar, p. 305.
92. Read about this anecdote in: *Early Writings*, Vol. III, p. 62.
93. Mary Lutyens, *Fulfillment*, p. 157.
94. See, among others: Lutyens, *Door*, p. 80, 88. Additional and somewhat awkward documentation of the conflict between Krishnamurti and Rajagopal is presented in Radha Rajagopal Sloss' biography on Krishnamurti. For an outsider, it is nearly impossible to judge the behavior of the two main characters. While Radha Rajagopal Sloss sees her father more in the role of the victim, the persons involved on Krishnamurti's side evaluate it quite differently. As Mary Lutyens told me by telephone after the Sloss-biography was published, she is preparing a response which might shed more light on these events. However, one fact can be stated now. The money that KWINC received under the management of Rajagopal was generated by Krishnamurti's intellectual property. Therefore, it seems only fair for Krishnamurti to request that he sit on the board of the establishment that manages said property. This was a moral right, independent of any arrangements that had been made beforehand.
95. Ibid., p. 131.
96. *Questions and Answers*, Krishnamurti Foundation Trust: London 1982, p. 88.
97. Alcyone, *At the Feet of the Master*, The Theosophical Publishing House: Wheaton, 1989, p. 20.
98. *Early Writings*, Vol. I, p. 92.
99. Mary Lutyens, *Awakening*, p. 127.
100. Rom Landau, *God is my Adventure*, Nicholson & Watson: London 1964, p. 206.

101. Mary Lutyens, *Door*, p. 94.

102. Landau, loc. cit., p. 215. See also Jayakar, loc. cit., p. 435 "'The teachings were not the book,' he said. 'The only teachings were, 'Look at yourself. Enquire into yourself—go beyond.' There is no understanding of the teaching, only understanding of yourself. The words of K were a pointing of the way. The understanding of yourself is the only teaching.'"

103. Landau, loc. cit., p. 216.

104. *Commentaries on Living*, Vol. II, 7th Edition, The Theosophical Publishing House: Wheaton, 1991, p. 126.

105. Mary Lutyens, *Door*, p. 69; see also: Krishnamurti, *World of Peace/ Die Welt des Friedens*, Jadrny Verlag: München, 1985, p. 157: "When you listen to K., he is not instructing you. He is putting up a mirror in front of you to see yourself. And when you see yourself very clearly you can break the mirror and be independent of the man who holds the mirror."

106. C. Vitelleschi, *Ethik als Tat*, Diederichs: Jena, 1930, p. 18.

107. *Early Talks*, Vol. II, p. 129.

108. *The Awakening of Intelligence*, Harper & Row: San Francisco,1973, p. 24.

109. Landau, loc. cit., p. 207.

110. Alcyone, p. 48.

111. Mary Lutyens, *Awakening*, p. 157.

112. *Commentaries on Living*, Vol. I, The Theosophical Publishing House: Wheaton, 1956, p. 19.

113. Emily Lutyens, p. 183. In this connection a remark about the three volumes of *The Initiate*, published anonymously by Cyril Scott, is adequate. In the second volume, two 'Masters' talk about Krishnamurti. "'Well, did my Brother Koot Hoomi say that

Krishnamurti had destroyed all the many stairways to God, while his own remains incomplete.'".
"'And would never be suitable *for all* types, in any case,' J. M. H. put in....".
"Sir Thomas nodded assent. 'And while he has directed them to repudiate all Masters, he refuses to act as Guru to them himself.' The old gentleman was silent for a moment, then shook his head mournfully. 'Children crying in the night of spiritual darkness, and no one to comfort them.... He who could help, won't, and we who might help, can't, for Doubt has poisoned their belief in our very existence. No wonder Koot Hoomi's face looks a little sad.'" Cyril Scott, *The Initiate in the Dark Cycle*, Samuel Weiser: York Beach, 1991, p. 138.

114. Emily Lutyens, p. 185. In this context, Rajagopal's request seems understandable and legitimate. Krishnamurti should have had more patience and understanding for those people who did not fully understand his breaking with the Theosophical Society (see Sloss, p. 135).

115. Mary Lutyens, *Life and Death*, p. 88.

116. Mary Lutyens, *Awakening*, p. 107.

117. Ibid., p. 305. Radha Sloss, too, reports a successful healing treatment through Krishnamurti which happened during her childhood (see Sloss, p. 258). Even though he was reluctant about it in public, he was open to use his healing powers in his private life.

118. Vimala Thakar, *On an Eternal Voyage*, Vimala Thakar Foundation: Holland, 1974.

119. Ibid., p. 31.

120. Ibid., p. 32.

121. Ibid., p. 40.

122. See Rom Landau, loc. cit., p. 76.

123. Jayakar, p. 6.
124. See also, among others: Jayakar, pp. 20, 27 and Mary Lutyens, *Awakening*, p. 5.
125. Mary Lutyens, *Awakening*, p. 305.
126. Mary Lutyens, *Door*, p. 92.
127. Ibid., p. 144.
128. Field, loc. cit., p. 48.
129. Ibid., p. 65.
130. Emily Lutyens, loc. cit., p. 68. See also the words of 'good bye' to Mary Zimbalist, which were meant seriously: "An Angel is accompaning you." Mary Lutyens, *Fulfillment*, p. 219.
131. Jayakar, p. 48.
132. Ibid., p. 53.
133. Mary Lutyens, *Life and Death*, p. 118.
134. See Mary Lutyens, *Fulfillment*, p. 186.
135. Jayakar, p. 155.
136. Mary Lutyens, *Fulfillment*, p. 120.
137. Jayakar, p. 229.
138. See *The Initiate in the New World*, loc. cit., p. 300. From a theosophical point of view, there is an interesting hint by David Anrias on this question, who explains some of Krishnamurti's peculiarities with his close connection to certain high Devas. David Anrias, *Through the Eyes of the Masters*, 8th Edition, Routledge & Kegan: London, 1976, p. 66.
139. Krishnamurti's remarks about the accusations in *The Initiate* can be found in *Early Talks*, Vol.IV, p. 100.
140. Mary Lutyens, *Fulfillment*, p. 207.
141. Mary Lutyens, *Fulfillment*, p. 69.
142. See Mary Lutyens, *Life and Death*, pp. 130, 151.
143. Mary Lutyens, *Awakening*, p. 202. See also Jayakar, p. 53 and E. Lutyens, p. 103.

144. As Dora Kunz, who was the only person present during those discussions between Leadbeater and Krishnamurti, explained to me, Leadbeater said the same things in private circles as well. At that time, Dora Kunz had the impression that he did not intend to influence Krishnamurti in any way. According to Mary Lutyens, Leadbeater's silence or uncertainty had been "more a proof of his clarity than the contrary"(Mary Lutyens, *Awakening*, p. 200).

145. Gopi Krishna, *Living with Kundalini*, Shambhala: Boston, 1993 (especially p. 32, p. 142).

146. Jayakar, p. 56.

147. Ibid., p. 242.

148. Ravi Ravindra, *The Mill and the Mill-Pond*, Krishnamurti Found. of America: Ojai, (no year), p. 4.

149. Jayakar, p. 131.

150. *Krishnamurti's Notebook*, p. 28; See also Mary Lutyens, *Fulfillment*, p. 180.

151. Jayakar, p. 489.

152. See Marianne Ryzek, *Über K.*, Edition Geflechte: Eurasburg, 1985.

153. Jayakar, p. 71. For an interesting detail about one of Krishnamurti's 'lives,' see *48 Lives* which deals with extra-physical experiences (Chap. XXXIV).

154. Jayakar, p. 83.

155. Mary Lutyens, *Life and Death*, p. 154.

156. Mary Lutyens, *Door*, p. 100.

157. See Mary Lutyens, *Fulfillment*, p. 232.

158. Ibid., p. 116.

159. Mary Lutyens, *Life and Death*, p. 118.

160. Jayakar, p. 438.

161. See Mary Lutyens, *Door*, p. 92. In 1927, Krishnamurti gave a talk in Eerde: "To me it (the Beloved, P.M.) is

all—it is Sri Krishna, it is the Master K. H., it is the Lord Maitreya, it is the Buddha, and yet it is beyond all these forms. What does it matter what name you give?... If I say, and I will say, that I am one with the Beloved, it is because I feel and know it"(Mary Lutyens, *Awakening*, p. 268).

162. Jayakar, p. 31.
163. See Mary Lutyens, *Life and Death*, p. 60.
164. See Mary Lutyens, *Fulfillment*, p. 34.
165. Jayakar, p. 405.
166. Ibid., p. 292.
167. Susunage Weeraperuma, *Krishnamurti as I Knew Him*, Chetana: Bombay 1988, p. 150.
168. Mary Lutyens, *Life and Death*, p. 136.
169. Ibid., p. 195.
170. Ibid., p. 206.
171. Ibid., p. 168.
172. *Early Writings* , Vol. III, p. 39. Krishnamurti also said in a conversation with P. Jayakar: "I have never asked myself what the mind is, the inner nature of K. If I reply 'nothing,' which means 'not a thing,' would that be acceptable? There is nothing. Would you comprehend the state of K's inner being, which is nothing, which is absolutely nothing? It is like measuring the immeasurable. I am not saying my mind is immeasurable—but it is like measuring the immeasurable." (Jayakar, p. 332)—As a simple remark, perhaps to help see things in relative terms, I add that in Pondicherry on November 24, 1926, only three years before those words were spoken, Aurobindo realized the coming of the 'Supramental,' a new, higher form of consciousness, which in his opinion manifested itself on earth for the first time (see K.R. Srinivasa Iyengar, *Sri*

Aurobindo, 4th Edition, Aurobindo Ashram Press: Pondicherry, 1985).

173. Mary Lutyens, *Life and Death*, p. 160.
174. Jayakar, p. 440.
175. Mary Lutyens, *Life and Death*, p. 188.
176. Jayakar, p. 498.
177. Ingram Smith, *Truth is a Pathless Land*, loc. cit., p. 120.
178. Radhika Herzberger in: Krishnamurti, *The Future is Now*, loc. cit., p. 20.

Part 2—The Teaching

179. *The First and Last Freedom*, p. 63.
180. *Krishnamurti to Himself*, p. 127.
181. See *Early Talks* , Vol. I, p. 147.
182. C. Vitelleschi, loc. cit., p. 18 (retranslated into English).
183. Additional information in *Early Works*, Vol. VII, p. 41.
184. See Mary Lutyens, *Awakening*, p. 282.
185. See Luis S. R. Vas (ed.), *The Mind of Krishnamurti*, 3rd Edition, Jaico Publishing House: Bombay 1975, p. 51.
186. See ibid, p. 91.
187. See J. E. Coleman, loc. cit., p. 75.
188. *The Kingdom of Happiness*, p. 58.
189. As in the meeting of the Trustees in Ojai 1977.
190. *The Ending of Time*, p. 31.
191. *Welt des Friedens/World of Peace*, p. 110.
192. *Freedom from the Known*, p. 119.
193. See *Bulletin 54*, Krishnamurti Foundation of America: Ojai, 1988, p. 7.
194. Jayakar, p. 192.

195. *The First and Last Freedom*, p. 207.
196. Jayakar, p. 193.
197. Renée Weber, *Dialogues with Scientists and Sages*, p. 67.
198. Rom Landau, loc. cit., p. 222.
199. *Early Writings*, Vol. V, p. 7.
200. See ibid., Vol.III, p. 22.
201. *Later Talks*, Vol. I, p. 99.
202. G. Hodson, *Krishnamurti*, loc. cit., p. 7.
203. *Early Works*, Vol. VII, p. 60.
204. *Commentaries on Living*, Vol. I, p. 213.
205. Mary Lutyens, *Awakening*, p. 282.
206. Ibid., p. 269.
207. *Collected Works*, Vol. I, p.105.
208. Jayakar, p. 415.
209. *Saanen 1st Public Talk*, June 6, 1980.
210. Jayakar, p. 392.
211. Ibid., p. 192.
212. *The Future is Now*, p. 152.
212a. Mabel Collins, *Light on the Path*, 4th Edition, The Theosophical Publishing House: Wheaton 1989, p.10.
213. Mary Lutyens, *Awakening*, p. 263.
214. See John White (ed.), *What is Enlightenment*, p. 97.
215. Alan Watts, *In My Own Way*, Vintage Books, Random House: New York, 1972, p. 136.
216. Wodehouse, loc. cit., p. 20.
217. See S. Field, loc. cit., p. 135; see also R. Weber, loc. cit., p. 225.
218. Emily Lutyens, loc. cit., p. 185.
219. Luis S. R. Vas, loc. cit., p. 55.
220. S. Field, loc. cit., p. 117.
221. Mary Lutyens, *Fulfillment*, p. 38.
222. Weeraperuma, *K. as I Knew Him*, loc. cit., p. 159.

223. Ibid., p. 108.
224. *Questions and Answers*, loc. cit., p. 150.
225. *Collected Works*, Vol. XIII, p. 195.
226. *Education and the Significance of Life*, p. 50.
227. *Education and the Significance of Life*, p. 25.
228. *Welt des Friedens/World of Peace*, p. 114.
229. V. Thakar, loc. cit., p. 12.
230. Mary Lutyens, *Door*, p. 45.
231. *The Flame of Attention*, p. 9.
232. *Welt des Friedens/World of Peace*, p. 16.
233. Ibid., p. 20.
234. Jayakar, p. 143; see also *Freedom from the Known*, p. 52.
235. *Commentaries on Living*, Vol. III, p. 230.
236. *Education and the Significance of Life*, p. 15.
237. *Krishnamurti To Himself*, p. 29.
238. S. Field, loc. cit., p. 92.
239. See Mary Lutyens, *Door*, p. 50.
240. Mary Lutyens, *Life and Death*, p. 94.
241. *Krishnamurti to Himself*, p. 10.
242. Jayakar, p. 236.
243. S. Weeraperuma, *K. as I Knew Him*, loc. cit., p. 33. He was more critical in a conversation with R. Weber; see *Dialogues with Scientists and Sages*, loc. cit., p. 224.
244. Jayakar, p. 237.
245. Ibid., p. 246.
246. *Education and the Significance of Life*, p. 18.
247. See Petra Michel (ed.), *Wissenschaftler und Weise—Die Konferenz,* loc. cit..
248. S. Weeraperuma, *K. as I Knew Him*, loc. cit., p. 69.
249. *Letters to the Schools*, Vol. I, p. 124.
250. *Krishnamurti to Himself*, p. 10. See also *Early Writings*, Vol. III, p. 103.
251. Weeraperuma, *K. as I Knew Him*, p. 32.

252. J. White, *What is Enlightenment*, loc. cit., pp. 93,100.
253. *The Only Revolution*, p. 89.
254. See *The Ending of Time*, p. 74.
255. J. White, p. 93.
256. *Talks and Dialogues*, p. 86.
257. *Saanen 1st Public Talk*, July 6, 1980.
258. See *The Future of Humanity*, p. 66.
259. See White, p. 141.
260. See *The Way of Intelligence*, p. 187.
261. Jayakar, p. 470.
262. Luis S. R. Vas, *The Mind of J. K.*, loc. cit., p. 82.
263. *Fredom from the Known*, p. 15.
264. *The Flame of Attention*, p. 26.
265. Jayakar, p. 430.
266. *Washington D.C. Talks 1985*, p. 50.
267. Mary Lutyens, *Door*, p. 58.
268. See G. Hodson, *Krishnamurti*, loc. cit., p. 13.
269. See Mary Lutyens, *Life and Death*, p. 120.
270. Ibid., p. 85.
271. Mary Lutyens, *Awakening*, p. 303.
272. *Early Writings*, Vol. I, p. 33.
273. *Early Writings*, Vol. IV, p. 71.
274. *Early Writings*, Vol. I, p. 122.
275. *Early Writings*, Vol. II, p. 6; see also Mary Lutyens, *Fulfillment*, p. 22.
276. *Early Writings*, Vol. II, p. 28.
277. Ibid., p. 191.
278. E.A. Wodehouse, *A Conversation...*, loc. cit., p. 24.
279. Carlo Suares, *K. and the Unity of Man*, 6th Edition, Chetana: Bombay, 1982, p. 204.
280. For similar thoughts see Jayakar, p. 371.
281. *The Future of Humanity*, p. 10.
282. *Krishnamurti's Journal*, p. 51.

283. *The Way Of Intelligence*, p. 187.
284. Ibid., p. 171.
285. *Krishnamurti's Notebook*, p. 28.
285a. About morphogenetic fields, see: Rupert Sheldrake, *A New Science of Life*, J. P. Tarcher: Los Angeles, 1981; ibid., *The Presence of the Past*, Random: New York, 1989; ibid., *Rebirth of Nature*, Bantam: New York, 1992.
286. *The Awakening of Intelligence*, p. 23.
287. Mary Lutyens, *Life and Death*, p. 191.
288. See his conversation with Scott Forbes in 1985; Mary Lutyens, *Door*, p. 113.
289. Jayakar, p. 436.
290. See Emily Lutyens, p. 26; see also Jayakar, p. 143.
291. Jayakar, p. 441.
292. See Emily Lutyens, p. 185 and Mary Lutyens, *Fulfillment*, p. 77. On this topic, Krishnamurti's conversation with Suares is also interesting; see Vas, loc. cit., p. 94.
293. At times, Krishnamurti's idea about resolving fears seems to have a touch of naïveté; see *Early Writings,* Vol. III, p. 99 or Jayakar, p. 249.
294. Mary Lutyens, *Life and Death*, p. 151.
295. Jayakar, p. 300; see also *Washington D.C. Talks 1985*, pp. 23, 28.
296. *Collected Works*, Vol. XVI, p. 213.
297. *Education and the Significance of Life*, p. 43.
298. See Jayakar, p. 257.
299. See *The Flame of Attention*, p. 66.
300. *Education and the Significance of Life*, p. 58.
301. See I. v. Massenbach, *Ausgewählte Texte*, p. 188.
302. *Talks and Dialogues in Saanen 1968*, (retranslated into English).
303. *Welt des Friedens / World of Peace*, p. 14.

304. Mary Lutyens, *Life and Death*, p. 78, and Mary Lutyens, *Awakening*, p. 296.
305. *Collected Works*, Vol.I, p. 34.
306. *The Second Penguin Krishnamurti Reader*, p. 236.
307. *The Flame of Attention*, p. 29.
308. *Talks and Dialoguess in Saanen 1968*, p. 24.
309. *Education and the Significance of Life*, p. 59; see also Mary Lutyens, *Life and Death*, p.149.
310. Mary Lutyens, *Life and Death*, p. 191.
311. Jayakar, p. 218.
312. *Talks with American Students*, p. 96.
313. Jayakar, p. 399.
314. *Later Talks*, Vol. 1, p. 128.
315. *Freedom from the Known*, p 19.
316. Balfour-Clarke, loc. cit., p. 21; see also Krishnamurti's moving words, written a few days after the death of his brother, about the "great love which is permanent, imperishable and unconquerable." In Mary Lutyens, *Awakening*, p. 239.
317. Vimala Thakar, loc. cit., p. 40.
318. Jayakar, p. 259.
319. Ibid., p. 133. Taking this into account, it is difficult for me to belief, as Radha Sloss writes, that Krishnamurti hated his father (see Sloss, p. 313).
320. *Talks with American Students*, p. 126.
321. *Talks and Dialogues Saanen 1968*, p. 105.
322. *Notebook*, p. 206.
323. Rom Landau, loc. cit., p. 213. This statement should be qualified in view of later developments. Krishnamurti's relationship to Rosalind Rajagopal, probably one of his earliest sexual relationships, carries strong aspects of normal personal love. What Rosalind probably never understood, and her daughter

Radha's book supports this assumption, was that Krishnamurti, even when he felt personal love, lived in his spiritual reality, in a different dimension. One could not hold on to Krishnamurti, even if he loved from the level of his personality. Neither was his love excluding, as becomes apparent in his feelings for Rajagopal during the first years of Krishnamurti's relationship with his wife Rosalind. Reading the Sloss biography carefully, one realizes that she had difficulties with this quality of Krishnamurti. To me, her accusation that Krishnamurti was hypocritical seems rather to reflect her misunderstanding of all-encompassing love (see Sloss, pp. 134, 262, and 308).

324. Emily Lutyens, *Candles*, p. 185.
325. A. J. G. Methorst-Kuiper, loc. cit., p. 61.
326. Jayakar, p. 313.
327. Ibid., p. 83.
328. J. White, *What is Enlightenment*, p. 105. See also in *Commentaries on Living*, Vol. I, p. 185: "As you have seen, love is not thought. Love is when the thinker is not. The thinker is not an entity different from thought; thought and thinker are one. The thinker is the thought."
329. Mary Lutyens, *Life and Death*, p. 118.
330. *The Second Penguin Krishnamurti Reader*, p. 173.
331. *Freedom from the Known*, p. 82.
332. Mary Lutyens, *Life and Death*, p. 170.
333. Jayakar, p. 307.
334. Ibid., p. 253.
335. Landau, p. 74.
336. *Washington D.C. Talks 1985*, p. 42.
337. Jayakar, p. 253.
338. Mary Lutyens, *Life and Death*, p. 85. I do not think Mary Lutyens' assumption that Krishnamurti used his

healing power "only rarely" is correct. See Mary Lutyens, *Door*, p. 71.

339. Vimala Thakar, loc. cit., p. 31; see also ibid., p. 36.
340. See Mary Lutyens, *Door*, p. 125.
341. See Weeraperuma, *K. as I Knew Him*, loc. cit., p. 84.
342. R. Field, loc. cit., p. 122.
343. Jayakar, p. 157.
344. Vimala Thakar, loc. cit., p. 32.
345. See Rohit Mehta, *The Intuitive Philosophy*, 3rd Edition, Motilal Banarsidass Publishers: Bombay, 1988, Preface.
346. Jayakar, p. 172.
347. *Early Writings*, Vol. III, p. 6; see also his poems in *Collected Works*, Vol. I, pp. 22, 51.
348. *Early Writings*, Vol. IV, p. 69; see also Methorst-Kuiper about Krishnamurti's view on the 'Lives of Alcyone,' which are described as correct in the general ideas but incorrect in the details.
349. *Early Writings*, Vol. IV, p. 75; see also in this connection *Early Writings*, Vol. V, p. 141 as well as the interview by Gladys Baker, in the *Birmingham Herald*, and *The Awakening of Intelligence*, p. 413.
350. *Talks with American Students*, p. 129.
351. *The Future is Now*, p. 87.
352. *Early Writings*, Vol. V, p. 110.
353. *Early Writings*, Vol. IV, p. 71; see also Mary Lutyens, *Life and Death*, p. 20.
354. Mary Lutyens, *Awakening*, p. 173.
355. See ibid., p. 305.
356. S. Field, p. 125.
357. Jayakar, p. 380; see also Mary Lutyens, *Fulfillment*, p. 219.
358. Mary Lutyens, *Door*, p. 92.

359. Jayakar, p. 364.
360. Weeraperuma, *K. as I Knew Him*, p. 80.
361. Ibid., p. 153. In his talk with Weeraperuma, Krishnamurti is even more clear when he says: "The future cannot be predicted" (p. 154).
362. *Early Writings*, Vol. IV, p. 154.
363. Mary Lutyens, *Awakening*, p. 171.
364. *The Kingdom of Happiness*, p. 91.
365. Jayakar, p. 211.
366. *Krishnamurti's Journal*, p. 63.
367. *Exploration into Insight*, p. 90.
368. Weeraperuma, loc. cit., p. 150.
369. In this direction, Rodney Fields reported a charming anecdote about Krishnamurti rescuing a beetle (p. 121).
370. Jayakar, p. 414.
371. *Krishnamurti's Notebook*, p. 218.
372. *Collected Works*, Vol. XIV, p. 180.
373. *Krishnamurti's Journal*, p. 67.
374. *Early Writings*, Vol. VI, p. 101.
375. Mary Lutyens, *Awakening*, p. 170.
376. *Krishnamurti's Notebook*, p. 27. See also a part of a conversation with David Bohm: "One night in India I woke up; it was a quarter past twelve, I looked at the watch. And—I hesitate to say this because it sounds extravagant—the source of all energy had been reached. And that had an extraordinary effect on the brain. And also physically. I'm sorry to talk about myself, but, you understand, literally, there was no division at all; no sense of the world, of 'me.' You follow? Only this sense of a tremendous source of energy" (*The Ending of Time*, p. 18).
377. *The Network of Thought*, p. 67. See also Krishnamurti's answer published in the *Krishnamurti Bulletin*: "We

say that you—if you change yourself through freeing insight—transmit it to the whole consciousness. It happens. The great rulers of this world and the great killers of this world have influenced the human consciousness: Attilla, Ghengis Khan, Napoleon, Hitler and on the other hand Buddha and others. They influenced the human mind, the human consciousness" (*Bull.* 46/1984, p. 13; retranslated into English).

378. Weeraperuma, loc. cit., p. 43.
379. *Krishnamurti's Notebook*, p. 39.